ISLAND
HOTEL STORIES

© 2003 Assouline Publishing
601 West 26th Street, 18th Floor
New York, NY 10001 USA
Tel.: 212 989-6810 Fax: 212 647-0005
www.assouline.com

Translated from French by Diana Stewart

ISBN : 2 84323 448 4

Color separation: Gravor (Switzerland)
Printing by Grafiche Milani (Italy)

FRANCISCA MATTÉOLI

ISLAND
HOTEL STORIES

ASSOULINE

CONTENTS

Introduction 7

TASMANIA (Australia), *Errol Flynn,* Freycinet Lodge 8

MOTU TANE (Bora Bora), *Paul-Émile Victor,* Private Island 14

KEY WEST (Florida), *Tennessee Williams,* The Gardens Hotel 22

STROMBOLI (Isole Eolie), *Ingrid Bergman and Roberto Rossellini,* Sirenetta Park Hotel 28

ÎLE DE CHANTEMESLE (Paris area), *Claude Monet,* Chantemesle 36

MUSTIQUE (The Grenadines), *Princess Margaret,* The Cotton House 44

ROBINSON CRUSOE ISLAND (Chile), *Robinson Crusoe,* El Pangal Hosteria 52

EILEAN DONAN (Scotland), *"Highlander",* Inverlochy Castle 60

HIVA OA (Marquesas Islands), *Jacques Brel,* Hiva Oa Hanakee Pearl Lodge 68

DOMINICAN REPUBLIC (Caribbean Sea), *Oscar de la Renta,* Punta Cana Resort and Club 76

MARTHA'S VINEYARD (Massachusetts), *"Jaws",* Charlotte Inn 82

CORSICA (France), *Henri Matisse,* Le Maquis 90

SEYCHELLES (Indian Ocean), *"Goodbye, Emmanuelle",* Fregate Island Private 96

VANUA LEVU (Fiji Islands), *Jean-Michel Cousteau,* Jean-Michel Cousteau Fiji Islands Resort 102

AMORGOS (Cyclades), *"The Big Blue",* Aegialis Hotel 110

NECKER ISLAND (Virgin Islands), *Richard Branson,* Necker Island 118

ARCHIPELAGO OF ZANZIBAR (Tanzania), *Evelyn Waugh,* Fundu Lagoon 124

SRI LANKA (Indian Ocean), *"Indiana Jones and the Temple of Doom",* The Dutch House Doornberg 130

KUNFUNADHOO (The Maldives), *Sonu and Eva Shivdasani,* Soneva Fushi Island Resort 136

BALI (Indonesia), *Noel Coward,* Begawan Giri Estate 144

FIJI (Oceania), *"The Blue Lagoon",* Turtle Island 152

ST. BARTHELEMY (Guadeloupe), *Eric Tabarly,* Hôtel Saint-Barth Isle de France 160

PHUKET (Thailand), *"The Beach",* The Chedi Phuket 166

IBIZA (The Baleares), *"More",* Hotel Hacienda - Na Xamena 174

TAPROBANE (Sri Lanka), *Paul Bowles,* Taprobane Island 180

BAHAMAS (Atlantic Ocean), *"For Your Eyes Only",* Pink Sands Hotel Resort 186

HAWAII (Polynesia), *Jack London,* Four Seasons Resort Hualalai 192

BORA BORA (French Polynesia), *"Mutiny on the Bounty",* Bora Bora Lagoon Resort 198

Photographic Credits and Bibliography 206

Acknowledgments 208

To Bertrand

INTRODUCTION

Everyone has a captivating story about the islands hidden away somewhere. Mine start with my parents in the Fifties. At the time, they lived in Chili and often used to dine at a famous restaurant in Santiago, namely "La Bahia", *Calle Monjitas*. The restaurant not only entertained South Americans of course - Pablo Neruda, the Chilean Nobel Prize winner was a regular along with politicians and artists, but also visiting international celebrities including Clark Gable, Tyrone Power, Walter Pigeon and Douglas Fairbanks Jr. They all went to La Bahia to sample its renowned specialty, those famous *langostas*, the quite unique (rock) lobsters caught only a few kilometers from the restaurant, off the shores of the Juan Fernandez Islands. Customers sat down at tables beneath caricatures of the Jet Set and photographs of stars of the time, and began their sumptuous meal with a house cocktail, either a *Sputnik* or *Pecado original* (original sin), before ordering the irresistible *ostras al caldo de tortuga* (oysters in turtle consommé). Then the famous *langostas* made their appearance. How many times have I heard tales of these famous lobsters and these mysterious islands! I found out only much later on that one of these islands had sheltered the real Robinson Crusoe, the sailor who was the inspiration for Daniel Defoe's legendary novel. As for me, I used to imagine these modest fishermen leaving their mysterious piece of land, busy with their baskets, a hundred miles away from ever imagining that the fruit of their labors was famous as far away as Hollywood. Now, whenever I hear people talking about *Gone with the Wind*, I can easily conjure up the picture of Rhett Butler with a plate of rock lobster from these Chilean islands, in front of him.

To leave everything, to go and live somewhere else, far away, very far away, yet all alone. The islands possess all of these alluring dreams of isolation, of remoteness, of getting away from it all, of hiding, of escaping, of overcoming again, anything that anyone could possibly dream of. Just at the very mention of the word, one feels overwhelmed by a sensation of ultimate freedom that already separates these wonderful, intriguing islands from the rest of the world. A figment of our imagination? Some have made the break, for a while or forever. Many have often waited until the end of their life and have ended up by changing all their habits, by adapting themselves to this pocket-sized world, developing qualities of which they were previously totally unaware of, opening up their minds to embrace another logic, often starting again from scratch. As Paul-Emile Victor used to say, you must have the courage to cut all ties. Whether they are voluntary exiles or not, whether their island is famous or a secret whisper, whether it is a large plot of land or a piece of confetti; in the end these are issues of little importance. All those who have embarked on this adventure have revealed themselves to themselves, creating a unique world on these territories that escapes convention, performance, the rat race. Everyone tells their story in their own way, often very simply, without taking any credit whatsoever, but at the end of the day, all have the same message that was summarized to perfection by Jacques Brel: "I finally found some peace here".

Francisca Mattéoli

TASMANIA

(AUSTRALIA)

ERROL FLYNN

• FREYCINET LODGE •

There is something about the islands that you simply cannot shake off, a longing that remains part of you and the only cure for this ailment is to return. Errol Flynn's passionately interesting souvenirs are on this account both as revealing as poignant. As we discover that this outstanding example of Hollywood's Golden Age had every reason to end his days living the life of a free spirit aboard his even more famous four-mast *Zaca*.

Errol Flynn was born in Hobart, at the foot of Mount Wellington, in Tasmania, and spent his life dreaming of an ideal haven of peace, far away from the lights of the dream machine. He inherited his flamboyance, his zeal for freedom and his taste for adventure from this country. Kicked out of every school, he was a gold prospector, reporter, diamond smuggler, and buccaneer amongst the swashbucklers. His first appearance in a movie was playing the part of Christian Fletcher in an Australian remake of the *Bounty* mutiny. Prior to this, he had "knocked around" quite a lot. "I spent my early childhood in this rather intriguing and cold part of Southern Australia". His father was a zoologist and marine biologist, and his mother was a sailor's daughter. From a very early age, Errol Flynn accompanied his father on his search for rare species, camping with him under the stars, scrutinizing isolated streams and rivers "under the microscope". "We went off towards the west coast, to uneven land scattered with mammoth fossilized trees and there we hunted

Tasmanian tigers, an animal so rare that my father spent four years before catching one. Sometimes we traveled inland when he went on one of his scientific expeditions". Tasmania is the only country in the world where you can still find prehistoric animals like the Tasmanian tiger and the Tasmanian devil. Errol Flynn's father had several of them at home, as well as kangaroo rats, opossums and sheep. One day, his school organized a trip to sea. Errol Flynn was subjugated. "It was fascinating to see what was being fished up out of the depths – spiders, sea anemone, giant crabs, and torpedo fish". His grandfather, the Captain, also fed his passion for the ocean with his tales of pirates and buccaneers that the young boy eagerly listened to, with his ear glued to the door when the old man came to visit the house with his sailor friends. This yearning for adventure was something that never left him. As soon as he got to Hollywood where his looks caused a

Interior of the "Zaca".

Errol Flynn and his friend Howard Hill during a scientific expedition aboard the "Zaca", in 1946.

sensation, he constantly sought to recapture his childhood emotions once again, with his first boat the *Sirocco*, and then with the fabulous *Zaca*, that he purchased in 1944 and kept until his death. After *Captain Blood*, *Robin Hood*, and other massive box office hits, he fled from Majorca to the French Riviera to Jamaica, lived on his boat, shot fewer and fewer movies, drank more and more, forgot he was broke for a while when posing for glossy magazines of the time, at the helm with an old pipe and

the beard of a trooper. The first photos taken on board the *Zaca* were a fantastic tribute to Hollywood, to the dream, to elegance and to adventure. To the world of his childhood also, indubitably reflected forever in that gaze still riveted to that far distant horizon. The Tasmania that Errol Flynn knew has kept all its force, its mystery and its incongruity. Land of the aborigines well before the rising waters separated it from the Continent, discovered in 1642 by the Dutchman Abel Tasman, a British colony and a peni-

Freycinet Lodge and its bush cabins at the tip of Freycinet Peninsula.

tentiary colony, it became an Australian State in 1901 and is today classified in UNESCO's list of World Heritage sites. On the east coast, in the fantastic Freycinet National Park, two hours by road from Hobart via the Tasmanian Highway with unforgettable panoramic views revealed at each turn of the road, nestles "Freycinet Lodge". Most certainly a hotel, but above all representing a tremendous accomplishment for the preservation of nature. From far off, the Lodge can hardly be seen, only the pure waters, the beach, the bush. The pink mountain's color comes from the gra-nite. You have to go right up to the end of the peninsula to be able to catch a glimpse of the discreet pier overlooking the sparkling azure, blue sea and the main building in the bush. Around it, sixty wooden bush cabins just like small private houses have been distributed throughout the area, sufficiently isolated from one

another, delightfully rustic, and intentionally subdued. A wooden pathway also goes all around the property and is beautifully lit up in the evening. Neither television nor telephones are in the cabins. There is nothing to distract you from the surrounding array of splendid wild nature. The atmosphere is relaxed, cozy and sportive, with numerous magnificent hiking trails, and everywhere the sight of nature is effortlessly in evidence. There are black swans, sea eagles, wallabies, penguins, whales, dolphins, opossums and Tasmanian devils, a type of baby bear with an ogre's appetite! But also, there are wild orchids, acacias, orange and bright green lichens. From the hotel a thousand activities are possible: trekking, bird watching, flora and fauna watching, walks with guides who are very keen on history and geography, days in the peninsula's vineyards, excursions by Land Rover, walks to the tiny vil-

12

lage of Coles Bay, paddling around the sandy beaches and rocky outcrops in a kayak. At the end of the journey, you can conclude your day, tired but happy, sitting in front of a plate of fresh salmon that has only just been caught and a glass of sauvignon blanc.

Ron Richardson, an extensive traveler himself, opened the original resort, called "The Coles Bay Chateau", on this site in 1934. He thus contributed to making this Australian extremity of the world internationally renowned. As the island was originally discovered by the French, the place has been renamed after the French explorer Louis Freycinet who came here between 1802 and 1804. Since then Freycinet Lodge has enticed all those truly intrepid nomads who still want to experience an adventure. To understand what it was that Errol Flynn missed so much, you only have to take a look around you.

FREYCINET LODGE
FREYCINET NATIONAL PARK
COLES BAY – TASMANIA, 7215
AUSTRALIA
TEL.: + 61 (3) 6257 0101
FAX: + 61 (3) 6257 0278
stay@freycinetlodge.com.au
www.freycinetlodge.com.au

Freycinet cabin (one room) at $240,
Oyster Bay cabin (two rooms) at $310,
Wineglass cabin (with private spa) from $265 to $370.
Bay restaurant, Richardson's Bistro, Hazards Bar,
tennis courts, various excursions organized…

How to get there
From Hobart international airport, take the Tasman Highway (A3) with spectacular views of Freycinet peninsula. Thirty minutes after Swansea, turn right onto Coles Bay Road (C302).

MOTU TANE
(BORA BORA)

PAUL-ÉMILE VICTOR

• PRIVATE ISLAND •

Paul-Emile Victor in Bora Bora.

Of course, there was Antarctica, Lapland, Alaska, the Scandinavian routes, the enduring but amazing adventures the French Polar Expeditions that he created. An audacity, determination and staggering progressiveness that would have earned him a place between Sir Hillary and Thor Heyerdhal in the portfolio that *Vanity Fair* dedicated in 2002 to the world's greatest explorers. In 1934, accompanied by three companions, Paul-Emile Victor spent a year with the Ammassalik Eskimos. In 1936, he crossed the icy desert of Greenland on foot and by dog sleigh with three friends, before settling down alone for fourteen months with an Eskimo family. During the Forties, he became an American citizen, joined the US Air Force, designed equipment for mountain troops in

Colorado and, with the 'Search and Rescue' squadron, assisted aircrafts in difficulty. Later on, he founded a group for the Defense of Mankind and the Environment with, amongst others, Jacques-Yves Cousteau. He was an explorer, writer, poet, artist, designer, and environmentalist before his time. To celebrate his eightieth birthday, in 1987, he naturally returned to the land of Adelia.

"Live as you dream if you do not want to end up dreaming while living" he used to say. A phrase that could sum up this amazing man. Predestined to take over his father's pen and pipe factory, he devoured adventure stories and by the time he was thirteen he already knew what he wanted to do in life. "I wanted to be an explorer". He started off by working in his father's factory, and learnt a

Paul-Emile Victor on his "motu" Tane in August 1984.

very precious lesson there "how to communicate with mankind". He also acquired the remarkable faculty of adapting himself to any situation. At the time, his bedroom walls were covered with postcards of the islands. However, once he had convinced his parents to let him go, he set off to the North Pole first, for nearly thirty years. A vocation? Yes, without a doubt. But also, as he used to say, a way of not being "someone who just nods his head". His childhood dream of Polynesia was only achieved in 1976, at the age of sixty-nine, when he settled on the motu (small island) of Tane, the Isle of Man, in Bora Bora with his wife Colette and his son Teva. A new life at an age when others are shutting up shop. As a journalist so aptly said, the question was never "Why?" but "Why not?" Today Teva lives right nearby on his own motu, where he has opened a guest house with his wife, Vanessa, and talks about his life on the island with his mother and "PEV", as his friends called him, with a simplicity and a spontaneity that will make you want to go there. "In fact it was my mother who purchased the islet, in 1965 I think, and to begin with they went there several times a year to clear the land and to build a small 'faré' a house by the water, something quite basic. They

finally settled there after I was born, my father having calculated that in six months he had lost sixty percent of his time in travel, traffic jams, and car parking problems. Several other farés quickly followed. The main one, the punu faré (corrugated iron), was where we all gathered together for meals. The Teitei faré (high faré) was my father's office. My mother also had her own faré. My father spent all day in his suspended office, writing,

One of Teva Victor's sculptures.

The extraordinary way in which everything naturally adjusts itself.

drawing, and sculpting, as he was also a very good artist. My mother did all the physical work on the island, my father being twenty-five years her senior, and sixty-five years my senior, clearing the land, weeding and gardening, mechanical problems, engine and boat maintenance. Just as my wife and I do now on our own motu". One of his most striking memories: "If I needed to ask my mother something, I called her and she answered, 'I am here!' but as her voice came from somewhere in the middle of the 'motu' I had to look for her for a while before I found her hard at work, collecting coconut palm tree leaves, making fires or changing the electricity generator oil. I always knew where to find my father. He was behind his files, writing, but he always had time for me".

The terrace of Teva and Vanessa's guest "faré".

Teva and Vanessa settled on Haapiti Rahi motu, just a few minutes from the one where Teva's parents live. Their 'motu', over one hectare in size and entirely private, is surrounded by a multicolored lagoon. It is the Polynesian island one dreams of remote, preserved, invaded by coconut trees, exuberant ferns, 'tiaré', the suavely scented emblematic flower. From their "Private-Island", you can catch sight of Tane motu, protected by its exquisite coral barrier reef. Since 2001, they have entertained guests in a large, fully equipped 110-square-meter villa, located at one end of the island, just perfect for five people. They collect visitors by boat upon arrival in Bora-Bora. Everything is so very simple here. Vanessa cooks wonderfully and prepares the most delicious dishes, always using local produce, and then serving them either in the villa on the pretty terrace or on the beach. For those who wish, Teva is in contact with the best specialists to organize shark feedings, island tours by outboard canoe, or helicopter flights over the lagoon. With only a snorkel and mask, you will find more corals and varieties of fish than you could possibly imagine: multico-lored parrotfish, leopard rays, trumpet fish, surgeonfish, and diodons to name only a few. Well-selected books in the villa will take you around the world, whilst on the island you will live amongst Teva's splendid sculptures, just as he lived with his father's, made according to Polynesian tradition from coconut trees, coral detached by cyclones, or volcanic stones set down amidst the countryside. This is what is so enchanting and captivating. Unique memories, legends, the tropics, emotions, art and nature, the visible and invisible, the gentleness of life are all part of the reality of the island. Life there will not appeal to

everybody. But for those really looking to experience something else, who are sensitive to the essentials, "There is nowhere else in the world", as Paul-Emile Victor used to say when he talked about Polynesia. If going on a journey means changing your habits, opening the door to a new world, forgetting what you think you know, allowing your imagination to emerge and surprising yourself with your own discoveries, then Teva and Vanessa have indeed made their "Private Island" into a permanent voyage. Yes, truly, there is nowhere else in the world...

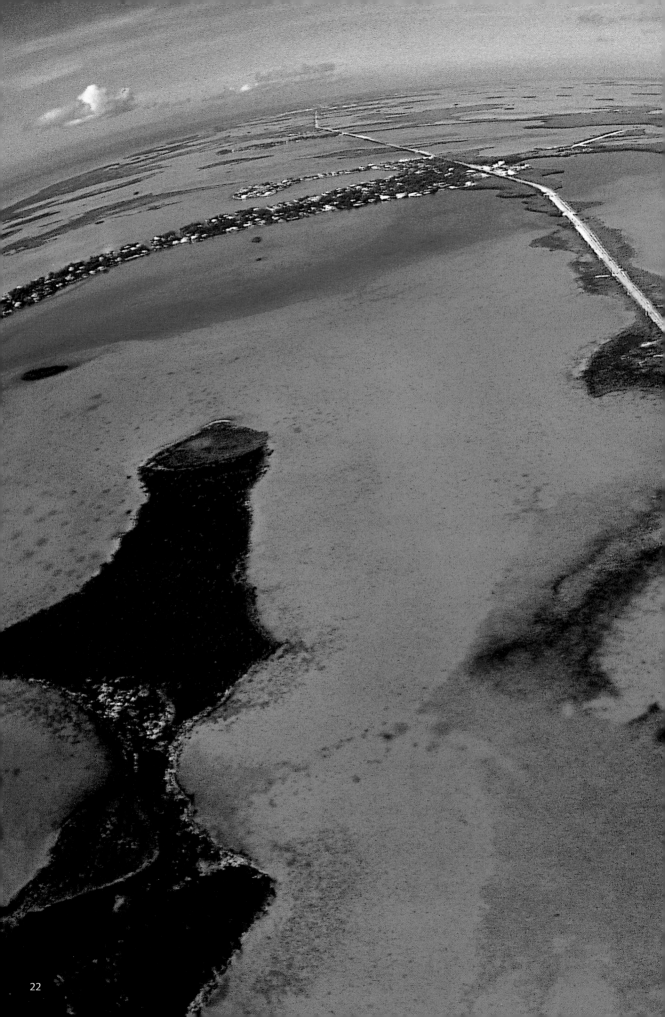

KEY WEST
(FLORIDA)

TENNESSEE WILLIAMS

• THE GARDENS HOTEL •

The very colonial Gardens Hotel.

Everyone who goes to Key West falls under its spell. On leaving Miami, you need to drive for a good four hours along the federal US 1 highway to reach this tiny wonder of American nature, but it's worth seeing. Everything here is so neat, pretty, elegant, and you will soon picture yourself in the shade on a beautiful verandah with a glass of pleasantly chilled wine in one hand.

The American Keys is a famous ribbon of islands that stretches out over 192 kilometers from Miami to Key West. The way there is truly a chef d'oeuvre of civil engineering with its forty-three bridges that span the islands. Key West is without a doubt the most well known of these. However, before you get to Key West there is Key Largo, the most mythical of them all, made immortal for all eternity by John Huston, Lauren Bacall and Humphrey Bogart. Key West is right at the end with its little wooden houses, its tropical, European atmosphere that is as relaxed as you can get, its pretty bars and its ravishing guesthouses full of plants. A hiding place and intellectual capital, Key West has captivated Hemingway, Dos Passos, Thomas Sanchez, Carlson Mac Cullers, and Tennessee Williams.

Tennessee Williams discovered Key West in 1941 on his way to Cuba. He was thirty years old at the time the ferry for Havana left from the Keys. His first play, *The Battle of the Angels,* was a complete flop in Boston and was only billed for two weeks in New York. He was not yet the great Tennessee but he already oscillated between phobias and neurosis. He initially came to Key West as a visitor with his lover and secretary Frank Merlo, a Sicilian-American he met in Massachusetts. It was only after the triumph of *A Streetcar Named Desire* that he bought a house there. This was to be the only fixed abode he would have for the whole of his life. "It was one of those rare spontaneous decisions of my existence" he used to say. "I love Key West. It is here that I work the best. I have decided to make it my home". His house is located in an unpretentious district on 1431 Duncan Street. After pushing open a small white gate and strolling along a

Tennessee Williams at Key West on May 3rd 1981.

24

short alleyway between the plants, you reach the discreet front door. Over the years, Tennessee added a swimming pool, a study reserved for writing and the Jane Bowles Summer House (named after his dear friend, the wife of the writer Paul Bowles). He settled there with his grandfather whom he adored, the Reverend Walter Dakin, who was half deaf and subsequently had his bedroom on the ground floor "because his conversations with the maid at the top of his voice when she arrived at 8 o'clock in the morning meant that it was impossible to sleep if you happened to be on the same floor", and with Frank Merlo who died there in the early sixties. He never recovered from this death. He became a sickly traveler, confusing partners with characters, who continued to go there, to entertain friends, trying as best he could to control his life, between nervous breakdowns and good times, alcohol and pills, sometimes helped by injections of vitamins from "Dr. Feelgood" alias Max Jacobson, the dubious doctor of celebrities of the time.

His house is still there, full of vegetation. It belongs to Maria St. Just, the writer's sole legatee who neither wants to sell nor allow visitors. And nearby, the heart of Key West continues to beat for writers and travelers with its little train, its charming Duval Street and Hemingway's

John Huston and Tennessee Williams during the shooting of "The Night of the Iguana" (1964).

The garden created by Peggy Mills at the "Gardens Hotel".

famous house. At The Gardens Hotel, near Duval Street, once again you will experience the atmosphere that fills the whole world with wonder. This handsome colonial house in the heart of the Historic District used to belong to Peggy Mills, nicknamed "The Lady of the Orchids" because she collected rare orchids from Hawaii and Japan. Passionate about plants, she devoted her whole life to creating the garden of her dreams. She created such an amazing place that when she departed, inhabitants of Key West came to "take away" her orchids so they would not die. These efforts have all worked together for our delight. An array of plants from all over the world surrounds the 1870 dwelling, in the National Registry of Historic Places, just like luxury trimming: Hibiscus, palm trees, jasmine, and species have attracted the botanists from all countries. Each moment liberates a

new scent ripened by the tropical moisture. The accommodation is elegant and intimate. Large balconies, soft colors, antiques and American handcrafted pieces in each of the rooms, every one differing in both splendor and beauty, all contribute to a feeling of well-being. The pretty fountains that spread throughout the garden numb the senses. One of the hotel barmaids, Barbara Bowers, is also a talented writer. She talks about her Key West in two delightful books *Once Upon an Island* and *Mango Summers*. In Key West, inspiration comes easily, freedom to do as you please, to dream dreams that surge up as you walk around, as everyone does, in shorts and sandals. Deep-sea fishing lovers are at home here. They only have to go down to the port to rent out a boat. Intellectuals are also at home here. Old Key West is full of historic houses and cultural walks. You can also sign up

for one of the writing courses organized all year round by the Key West Literary Seminar and the Key West Writer's Workshop. Finally, before returning home, do not miss a swim with the dolphins in the Dolphins Plus Center in Key Largo. An unforgettable experience. The Center also practices dolphin therapy, an increasingly widespread method which helps humans "in difficulty" by putting them in contact with the dolphins.

The Spaniards who discovered Key West in 1513 called it Cayo Hueso (Bone Island), a name that was later only to be phonetically anglicized. They never imagined it would become such a symbol of the genteel way of life. A feeling that The Gardens Hotel management would not deny, nor would Barbara Bowers, who has worked there for many years, writing and painting, surrounded by her cats, lizards and frogs.

THE GARDENS HOTEL
526 ANGELA STREET
KEY WEST, FL 33040
USA
SMALL LUXURY HOTELS OF THE WORLD
TEL.: + 1 (305) 294 2661
FAX: + 1 (305) 292 1007
reservations@gardenshotel.com
www.gardenshotel.com

12 rooms from $155 to $215 (off-peak season),
and from $265 to $355 (peak season);
4 suites from $175 to $485 (off-peak season),
and from $315 to $685 (peak season);
1 cottage from $295 during off-peak season
and from $465 during peak season.
Restaurant and bar, swimming pool,
open air spa, Peggy Mills's
botanic garden…

How to get there
From Miami, drive for approx.
4 hours (US1 Highway)
or take a 25-minute
domestic flight.

STROMBOLI
(ISOLE EOLIE)

BERGMAN
AND ROSSELLINI

• SIRENETTA PARK HOTEL •

Above: *The Sirenetta Park Hotel.*
Opposite: *Ingrid Bergman during the shooting of "Stromboli" (1949).*

The island is as disturbing as it is fascinating. There is something disconcerting in the raw ruggedness of the landscape, in the activity of Stromboli, in live volcano forever rumbling furiously, and in the striking, plain white houses at the foot of the furnace. Unsurprisingly the place has inspired artists and "fashionistas" to buy property here. There is something "rock n' roll" and avant-garde in this backdrop of blue sea set against black beaches of countryside suddenly illuminated by the flow of red lava, box-shaped houses and wild olive trees.

When Roberto Rossellini decided to shoot "Stromboli" in 1949, nobody had ever heard of this hidden corner of northern Sicily. "If you need to choose a coastal area that is beautiful, wild and legendary but, at the same time, as pleasing to the eye as it is enchanting to the soul, the Amalfitain coast is the perfect choice", wrote Ingrid Bergman in her souvenirs. The journey with the film crew started out on an idyllic note. The actress adored the wild, winding roads by the sea, and by the mountains. Traffic was rare at the time and the little villages were not used to seeing many tourists. The crew then set out for Stromboli with all the equipment in an old fishing boat. They sailed by the other islands, Lipari and Vulcano, and landed on Stromboli after two hours at sea. "At some 700 meters of altitude, the volcano was vomiting a flow of white smoke". The rest of the adventure was much less fun. In fact, the shooting was a nightmare for Ingrid Bergman. Roberto Rossellini wanted to portray the truth and therefore hence only used amateurs, island inhabitants who naturally knew nothing about acting. With no home comforts and only the bare necessities, the production did not have backing. The film crew even had to borrow money. In one scene, Ingrid Bergman had to climb up to the top of the volcano, and it took four hours to do so. Luckily, the adventure also had its good times. Roberto Rossellini had movies shipped over for the inhabitants of the island who had never seen any before, and he then projected on a screen set up in the village square. However, the boat that came from Naples with parcels also brought other news. Everyone on the set had noticed the more-than-professional relationship between the actress and the film director. The press seized on this information and published caricatures of the couple on the first page. Feminist and religious associations went crazy. Both of them were married and the scandal was colossal, resulting in the Motion Picture Association of America asking Ingrid Bergman to end these rumors. A member of the US Senate even called her "Hollywood's apostle of degradation". The public, accustomed to her looks in *Casablanca*, was not indulgent and Hollywood closed its doors to her.

31

Preceding double pages: *June 6, 1982 - Stromboli erupts ash and stream over the Tyrrhenian sea.*
Above: *Rossellini and Bergman on the volcano.*

The incident wrecked her American career. "People did not expect me to have feelings as other women do", said the actress.

Initially written for Ana Magnani, the role of Karin was given to Ingrid Bergman because she had sent an admiring letter to Roberto Rossellini saying that she would be happy to work with him. The movie tells the story of a young Lithuanian girl who decides to marry Antonio, a modest fisherman with whom she has nothing in common, in order to escape the concentration camps. He takes her home to his island, Stromboli, where she is a foreigner and, unable to adapt herself, resolves to run away. Against the backdrop of post-war Italy, the power of black and white, a magnificent Ingrid Bergman amidst lunar scenery, extremely savage tuna fishing, with that very poignant scene when she confronts the angry volcano to

no avail. The film is fascinating because of its realism, its silences, and its powerful images that you know are real. Moreover, it was the production coordinator of the movie who gave Aninna and Domenico Russo, teachers at the time, the idea of opening a hotel, seeing as to how the film unit had nowhere to stay. They started off by opening a trattoria in the Fifties with two guest rooms where volcano specialists such as Haroun Tazieff stayed. They then opened a proper hotel, the first one in Stromboli, now managed by their son Vitto Russo, a char-ming man with communicative good humor. Looking out onto the beach and the Tyrrhenian sea, the hotel is a credit to the family tradition with its attractive clusters of white houses, large swimming pool opposite the sea, olive trees spread between the terraces, pretty rooms overlooking the bay and restaurant-bar Le Tartana Club, a meeting place for

the whole island with fish dishes that use freshly caught fish of the day. Uncomplicated, warm and welcoming, the Sirenetta Park Hotel is constantly acclaimed for the qua-lity of its reception and spectacular location with breathtakingly beautiful surroundings. There are no cars in Stromboli. The narrow alleys were made for donkeys. You might be able to buy an old house here and reno-vate it but not to add any extensions. There is no out-side lighting apart from torches or flashlights. Boats regularly depart for the other islands such as the Eolians, Lipari, Salina, or Panarea, previously inhabited by the Dorians, Athenians, Carthaginians and Romans, and quoted in the Iliad and the Odysseus. A magical journey through countryside that is classified as world heritage by UNESCO. The pink house, where Roberto Rossellini and Ingrid Bergman stayed is still there, just after San Vicenzo church. Of course, climbing right to the top of Stromboli by night is a must. All necessary equipment can be provided in Stromboli, or from the village of Ginostra just behind, where you may also "have one for the road" next door in the restaurant, that last glass of Malvasia, a sweet local wine. Originally called Strongyle, "fiery spindle", this island was a natural lighthouse for sailors. Today Sirenetta's neighbors are Dolce and Gabbana.

SIRENETTA PARK HOTEL
VIA MARINA, 33
98050 STROMBOLI
ISOLE EOLIE,
ITALY
TEL.: + 39 (090) 986 025
FAX: + 39 (090) 986 124
lasirenetta@netnet.it
www.lasirenetta.it/pagine/home.htm

55 rooms and 2 suites from $70 to $238.
Restaurant and Tartana Club bar, swimming pool,
fitness center, tennis courts, diving center…

How to get there
From the international airport of Naples,
allow four hours by ferry.

ÎLE DE CHANTEMESLE

(PARIS AREA)

CLAUDE MONET

• CHANTEMESLE •

Preceding double pages: The legendary white water lilies and "The Artist's Garden at Giverny".
Above: *Monet's house in Giverny.*

Strictly speaking, Claude Monet was not at all unconventional. He grew a beard early on in life, adding a soft hat and a jacket to work in. He painted pictures of his house, garden and family. Yet this personality was truly an extremely unusual man, who worked away fiercely and unrelentingly, painting pictures of water for half of his life. Claude Monet discovered Giverny in April 1883. His childhood was spent in Le Havre; he had lived in Argenteuil, Poissy, and Vetheuil, always surrounded by water. He had experienced poverty before finally being able to secure a living that was more appropriate for his large family. He also finally had enough money to satisfy his dreams. He first set eyes on Giverny, a beautiful village in the department of Eure on the outskirts of Paris, one day whilst gazing out of a train window. He settled down without the slightest hesitation with his two sons, his second wife and her six children. Passionately fond of botany, he had always loved plants and flowers. He also admired Japanese etchings. He immediately started to create the things he had always dreamed of painting, his lake, his famous Japanese bridge, adding that tiny detail year after year, slowly but surely, aided by five gardeners, horticulturists and well known nurseries. He organized himself so that he could paint without leaving the water's edge, more or less. He purchased the tiny isle of Orties (stinging nettles), near the mouth of the river Epte, on the river Seine, had a hut built and, just as in Argenteuil, fitted out

a boat cum workshop, a little floating island on an old boat that very soon also found its way onto his canvasses. He beavered away from 5 in the morning, hypnotized, determined, traveling the length and breadth of the shores of the river Epte, the banks of the river Seine, the area surrounding Vetheuil, one of the most beautiful locations in the Seine Valley, searching for that special detail, for reflections in the water, for aquatic grass. "I have once again had a go at the sort of things that are practically impossible to portray. Things that are so wonderful to see but that will send you crazy if you attempt to paint them. In the end I always tackle such things!" he wrote to a friend. His incredible fascination provided him with subject matter for his work right up until the day he died at the age of eighty-six. As well as inspiration for the famous panels now at the Orangerie in Paris, the magnificent paintings that he started at seventy-six including his

The tiny boat that takes guests to Chantemesle.

Claude Monet in his garden at Giverny.

Peupliers, Matinées sur la Seine, La Seine à Vetheuil, Vetheuil sur l'eau, Automne sur la Seine, Les Glycines, Le Matin dans les Iles, Les Pommiers sur la Colline de Chantemesle, his famous white water lilies and irises, of course. This amateur of fine wine, who loved the good life, continued to work furiously and relentlessly, remai-ning enthusiastic right until the very end. His step-son, also a botanist, said that on the eve of his death Claude Monet was still waiting for the arrival of the lily bulbs that Japanese friends had promised him.

In Chantemesle, you will easily understand the artist's enthrallment and your only regret will be at not having brought a canvas and paintbrush along. It is rare that a place resembles the work it inspired such a long time afterwards. Chantemesle provides a very rare and quite extraordinary display. The humus, aquatic plants, reflections in the water on the river Seine, trailing wisteria, floating grass… Everything is there. It is sheer bliss to let

Chantemesle isle: the beautiful verandah of the main house.

yourself to slowly slip through this undulating countryside, just as in his masterpieces. Situated at the bottom of the famous Cretians route, between Vetheuil and Roche-Guyon, the island belonged to a doctor before a Belgian industrialist who was a yachting fanatic acquired it. "I always looked for houses near the water", he says. "When I was eight, my mother signed me up for a yachting course. This passion for water and boats have stayed with me since then". An amusing coincidence. After leaving the main road with its appealing cottages whose gardens are overflowing with flowers, you have to walk along a stony little path to reach the riverbanks. There someone will fetch you in a small boat that would have enchanted Monet. It glides along the water between the famous reflections, the grass, the water lilies, and taking you in just moments to reach the willow tree on the other side. Go up a few steps, pushing aside dripping branches, to a beautiful house with wooden walls, characteristic of the region. The décor is stunning. The six bedrooms in the main building all open onto a different part of the island and the enchanting parkland. The large Victorian style verandah is filled with the most delightful bits and pieces, merrily mingled together. It is warm, welcoming, and immediately friendly. There is a vegetable garden, an orchard, a path that starts off near a small alley of cream roses before losing itself in the incredibly dense under wood, a farmyard, a tennis court, a swimming pool, only a few yards from the river Seine so fanatically portrayed in paintings, a small beach much appreciated by both coypus and wild geese. The site is classified as a nature reserve and can be rented for a weekend, a week, or a month. Giverny, Monet's house and his famous museum are

nearby, as is the Roche-Guyon village, another picturesque treasure trove, with its ancient streets, second-hand furniture dealers chock-full of discoveries, along with a marvelous medieval château built against the cliffs. Vernon and Vetheuil, other villages out of time, are also nearby. Take the island's motor boat, following the gentle meanderings of the river Seine exactly as Monet did, dreaming of this extraordinary little island, all to yourself, barely thirty miles from the hustle and bustle of hectic Paris. Just heavenly...

ÎLE DE CHANTEMESLE
3, CHEMIN DE L'ABBAYE
HAUTE-ISLE
95 780 LA ROCHE-GUYON
FRANCE
TEL.: + 33 (6) 07 61 52 05
FAX: + 33 (1) 45 53 06 84
lang@noos.fr
www.chantemesle.com

Rental of the residence (maximum 10 guests)
for $3,251 (during off-peak season)
and $ 6,500 (during peak season) per week.
Orchard, vegetable garden, farm yard,
2 greenhouses, tennis court, swimming pool,
8 golf courses half an hour away
and riding school in close proximity...

How to get there
From Paris, take the Normandy highway,
exit at Mantes-la-Jolie East (junction n° 11).
Follow the direction of Limay via the D146,
then of Vetheuil on the D147, and La Roche-Guyon
along the D913. Upon arrival in Haute Isle,
take the cul-de-sac called "chemin de l'Ormeteau".
The car park is on your right, the landing pier on
your left – ring the bell on the letterbox
marked n° 3 to announce your arrival.

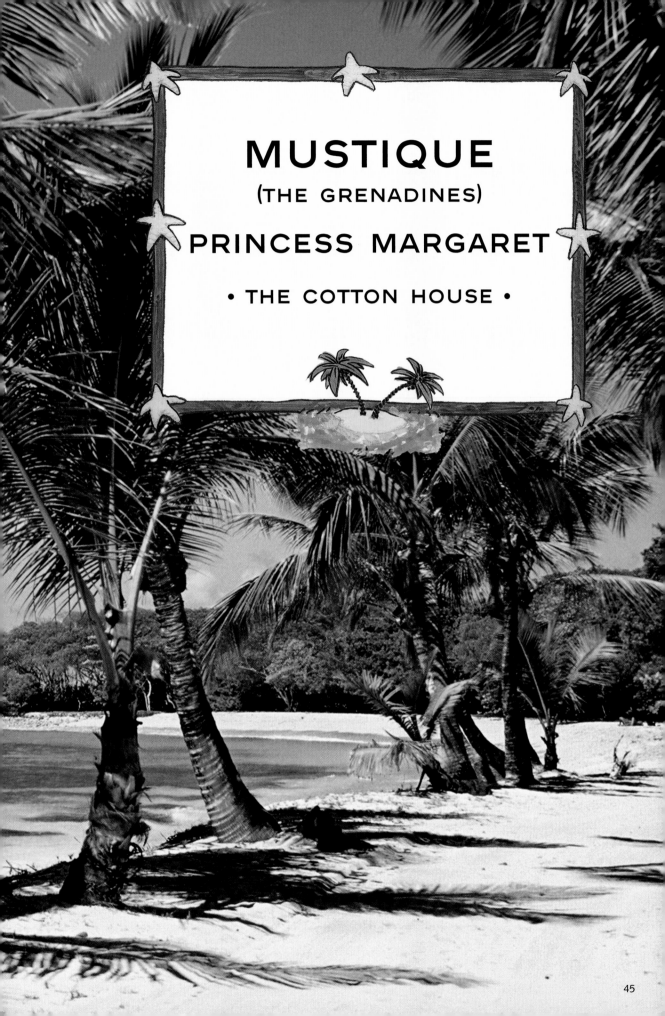

MUSTIQUE
(THE GRENADINES)

PRINCESS MARGARET

• THE COTTON HOUSE •

View of the seashore from The Cotton House hotel.

What can you possibly give a very good friend as a wedding present? A priceless vase? A silver frame? A few pieces of precious antiques? Lord Glenconner had a much better idea.

The story begins at the end of the Fifties. The Honorable Sir Colin Tennant, as Lord Glenconner was then known, a Scottish aristocrat and renowned eccentric, discovered a 1,400-acre island in the Grenadines, under attack by mosquitoes at that time. This little island, at about thirty minutes away by air from Martinique and Fort de France, had no home comforts. Only about a hundred people lived in the village then. Lord Glenconner, planted 125 hectares of island cotton and created a new village there. Then the swinging Sixties arrived with

parties, over-indulgence, a carefree atmosphere, The Beatles versus The Rolling Stones. His friends included Princess Margaret who also attended all the parties. She was seen with Peter Sellers, the Aga Khan, the writer Quentin Crewe, Rachel Welch, Mick and Bianca Jagger. She was young, admired, and emulated. She knew everyone, was used to going out every night and "The Margaret Set", as her group of friends was called, became the talk of the town. In 1960, she married the photographer Anthony Armstrong-Jones. No silver frame or priceless antique was good enough to celebrate such a momentous occasion, so Lord Glenconner gave her a ten-acre plot of land on the island he had acquired. A brilliant idea that suddenly made this little island

Above: *"Les Jolies Eaux", Princess Margaret's villa on Mustique.*
Opposite: *Princess Margaret and Lord Snowdon in March 1967.*

world-famous, and attracted both celebrities and royalty. Princess Margaret's villa was called "Les Jolies Eaux". Designed by the well-known decorator and London architect Olivier Messel, the villa affords the most fantastic view of the Grenadine Islands and the Caribbean Sea. The impulsive modern Princess Margaret, who loved clothes and jewelry, who made everyone who invited her to supper in London go crazy by always asking for something other than what had been prepared, was able to give free rein to these eccentricities. She said that she had as much private life as a goldfish in a bowl. A good enough reason to spend as much time as possible on the island she loved, with friends who knew her, and allowed her to lead a life where she was happy, to smoke as much as she wanted, to wear kaftans and turbans if she felt like it, to mix with rock stars, to go to bed at dawn, to do as she pleased. The ideal island, or nearly....

Olivier Messel also decorated The Cotton House, the hotel, which opened in 1969, as well as most of the villas on the island. A fabulous success that turned Mustique into one of the most exclusive islands in the Grenadines. The villa where Princess Margaret escaped to from London,and where she threw parties that never ended before dawn is now rented out, as are most of the villas on the island. Rental includes a jeep, gardener, cook, majordomo, and a private swimming pool. The dining room overlooks magical scenery that extends as far as "Canouan" or Turtle Island, and other spectacular islands in the Grenadines. It is a luxurious and very private retreat for secluded and highly sophisticated evenings. The documentary entitled *The Man Who Bought Mustique* is homage to this era. Lord Glenconner tells his story as well as of evenings where Princess Margaret, Jerry Hall, Bryan Ferry, Caroline Herrera, Mick and Bianca Jagger were all at the same party.

Mick Jagger in December 1983.

The Cotton House.

The Cotton House, the island's only hotel, was completely renovated a short while ago in keeping with the spirit of Olivier Messel and his famous clients. In countryside teeming with valleys surrounded by beaches, the former 18th Century planter's house has retained most of its original objects as well as its unique charm, making it one of the most beautiful hotels in the world. There are only twenty rooms, suites or cottages, of which the majority all have private terraces. The well-being of guests extends to offering them eleven different sorts of pillows (a firm pillow with feather heart, a pillow for a nap or even a maternity pillow!), a spa that makes you feel good just by reading about all the different massages on offer, an unpacking and ironing service provided to ensure you always have impeccable outfits, and household linen of Egyptian cotton. The hotel's catamaran,

The Mustique Mermaid, takes wave lovers off to discover the other wonders of the Grenadines, and on dry land the riding center proposes magnificent promenades. A picnic is a possibility, for which the hotel will provide you with one of their choice hampers to suit your individual tastes. Alternatively, have it taken down to you while you bathe on Lagoon Beach or Macaroni Beach. In another keeping with British tradition, "5 o'clock tea" is served every day in the Grand Salon that still has the original furniture designed by Olivier Messel, including a splendid cabinet completely decorated with shells.

There is only one tiny little port on the island, where a few small shops and the prettily named "Sweetie Pie Bakery" are to be found, as well as the delightful Basil's Bar, a bar-restaurant-boutique-nightclub actually on the water: a not-to-be missed legendary venue. Those who

come here never forget their very first visit, the sensation of perfect beauty and luxury right up to the subtle blue-green of the ocean, strewn with miniature havens such as Petit St. Vincent, or "PSV", right nearby, another divine plot of land turned into a hotel by a crazy adventurer. At Cotton House, refinement has been retained magnificently. For island residents, the hotel bar has always been the meeting place for cocktails. In addition to maintaining the tradition of Jet Set evenings and the exquisitely chic atmosphere of Mustique, the manager throws a cocktail party in the Main House every week.

GRENADIN
COTTAGE

The most mythical island in the world. Who does not know about it? What has not been written about it? Who has not been inspired to dream by it? Three centuries after the adventures of the real Robinson Crusoe, it continues to inspire books, films, paintings and a thousand meditations.

The story is most extraordinary. In 1703, Alexander Selkirk, a Scottish sailor, embarked as boatswain aboard an English boat. The twenty-four-year-old man was rather aggressive and soon had a fight with the captain. He asked to be disembarked on the first island they came to. This was Mas a Tierra (Nearer to Earth) off the Chilean coast, later to be known as "Robinson Crusoe's Island". He quickly regretted his choice and called out to be taken back on board. The Captain sent him the message, "You can starve to death on your island!" Thus, in 1704 he started his existence as a castaway with a Bible, a mathematics book, some measuring instruments, clothes, his gun and powder, the only means to light a fire and a few other articles he was allowed to keep, all of which had been deemed as potentially useful. They indeed proved to be so, considering that, contrary to his hopes, no boat approached the island for four years. He succeeded in surviving by hunting and fishing until a passing English boat took him back to England where his adventures were published in a magazine read by a writer named Daniel Defoe, who transformed this story into one of the most powerful and legendary literary myth of all time.

Since then, the theme has traveled all around the world: isolation, learning about another civilization, confrontation with oneself, survival in an unknown exotic place. It was quite impossible for the motion picture industry to allow such a scenario to escape unnoticed. In 1975, a Frenchman, Jean-Paul Rappeneau, visualized Robinson Crusoe played by Yves Montand, and gave him a dream partner played by the desirable Catherine Deneuve. Martin (Yves Montand) was a famous "nose" who left his job and his wife, manager of the perfume company who employed him, to spend a peaceful life on

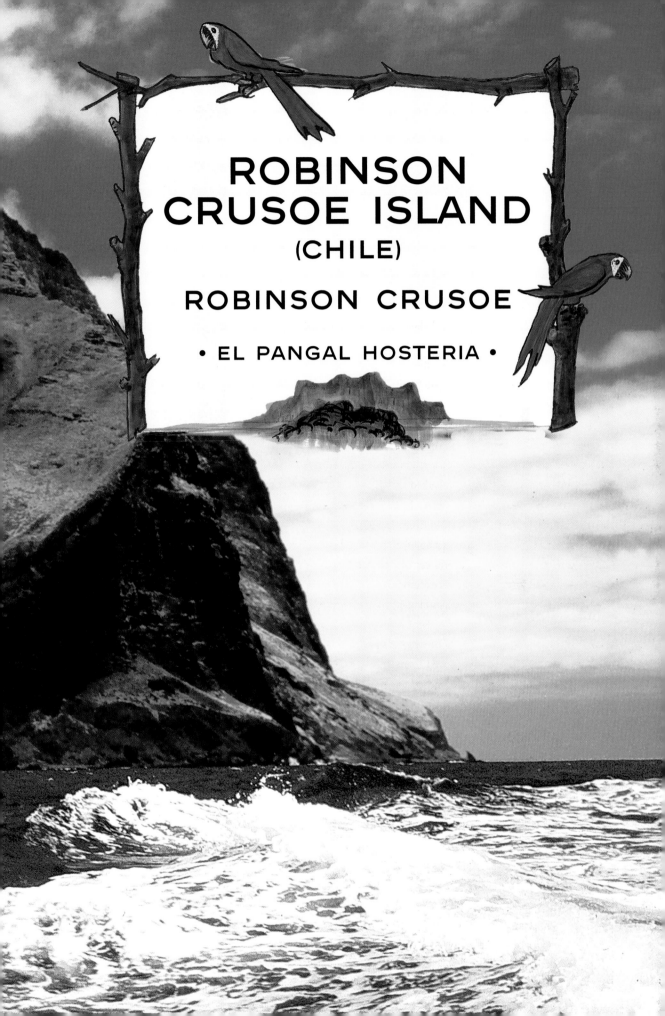

ROBINSON CRUSOE ISLAND
(CHILE)

ROBINSON CRUSOE

• EL PANGAL HOSTERIA •

an island off the coast of Caracas. His path crossed that of Nelly (Catherine Deneuve) who had fled her employer after stealing a Toulouse-Lautrec painting from him. Only too pleased to have found a French man at the other end of the world, and quite determined to make the most of her good luck, she followed him to his island. There could not have been two better actors for the role, combined with stunts, pursuits and magical settings. Deneuve with wet hair, sun-tanned bare legs, was fabulously sexy; Yves Montand as the irate Robinson had a three-day beard ... "I did not want to leave the atmosphere of the film", he said afterwards. An adventurous comedy in an idyllic setting that would have enchanted Howard Hawks and Frank Capra.

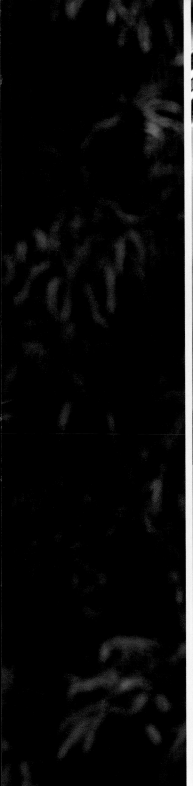

Tom Hanks in "Cast Away" (2000).

In 2000, it was Tom Hanks's turn to play Robinson in *Cast Away* directed by Robert Zemeckis. As a Federal Express Inspector, he traveled around the Pacific checking on the quality of deliveries. Following an aircraft accident, he became a cast away for several years on a desert island. He quickly learned how to survive and adapted to his new environment, reinventing the most basic skills, such as lighting a fire, finding drinking water and getting food... The shooting took sixteen months with a break of one year to enable Tom Hanks to change his physical appearance while the team went all over the Pacific Ocean to find the best location. The screenwriter even took a survival course to study what life on an island was all about, an adventure that Alexander Selkirk would have found

Preceding double pages: *El Pangal Hosteria.*
Above: *Commemorative plate on Alexander Selkirk Mirador.*

extremely amusing. The legend has been reinvented over a thousand times, until the ultimate adaptation, *Survivor*.... Robinson Crusoe's island. It was part of the Juan Fernandez Archipelago. Discovered in 1574 by the Spanish navigator Juan Fernandez, who arrived accompanied by sixty Indians, goats and chickens. After the battle of Rancagua in 1814, patriots were exiled. Transformed into a national park in 1935, it became a natural reserve, and today is classified by UNESCO as a World Biosphere Reserve. After a two-hour flight from Santiago above the endless Pacific Ocean, visitors arrive amidst wild life in its purest state. Alexander Selkirk survived here by hunting sheep and goats. Today the place is mainly full of rabbits. You can go as far as the promontory from where he scanned the horizon, hoping for the arrival of a boat. (In fact, two Spanish boats did go by, but he refrained from calling out to them as they augured hard labor mainly.) There is no airport on the island, only an earthen track and one solitary village, San Juan Bautista, where 600 people live. El Pangal Hosteria (or the place where the "pangal" grows, one of the island's typical plants) was built by Carlos Griffin, a visionary who was one of the first Chileans to land his aircraft there in 1966. It is located right in the middle of the forest, which houses tree species that remain unique throughout the world. The hosteria looks as if it has always been there in the middle of the mountains, covered with bronze-green grass and wild flowers. Built in the Eighties opposite the superb bay, it has retained its authentic quality, beautiful simplicity and an atmosphere that looks as if has just escaped from a *National Geographic* magazine. Wherever you look, your eyes are met by amazingly steep creeks, extraordinary

volcanic and jungle locations, amethyst blue-waters, giant ferns that are sometimes ten yards tall, emblematic trees, like the chonta, that only grows in a few places, rare animals and birds such as the famous Picaflor Rojo (Red Picaflor) or the double-coated wolf, whose fur kept Napoleon's army warm during his campaign in Russia. Travelers can visit sites that were dear to the cast away, and accompany anglers looking for the tastiest lobsters in the world to be prepared in an unforgettable *cazuela de langosta* (rock lobster fricassee). El Pangal also delights all guests with typical Chilean dishes served with one of the excellent red wines in the country and of course, a delicious *pisco*, the famous national aperitif.

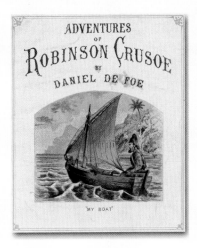

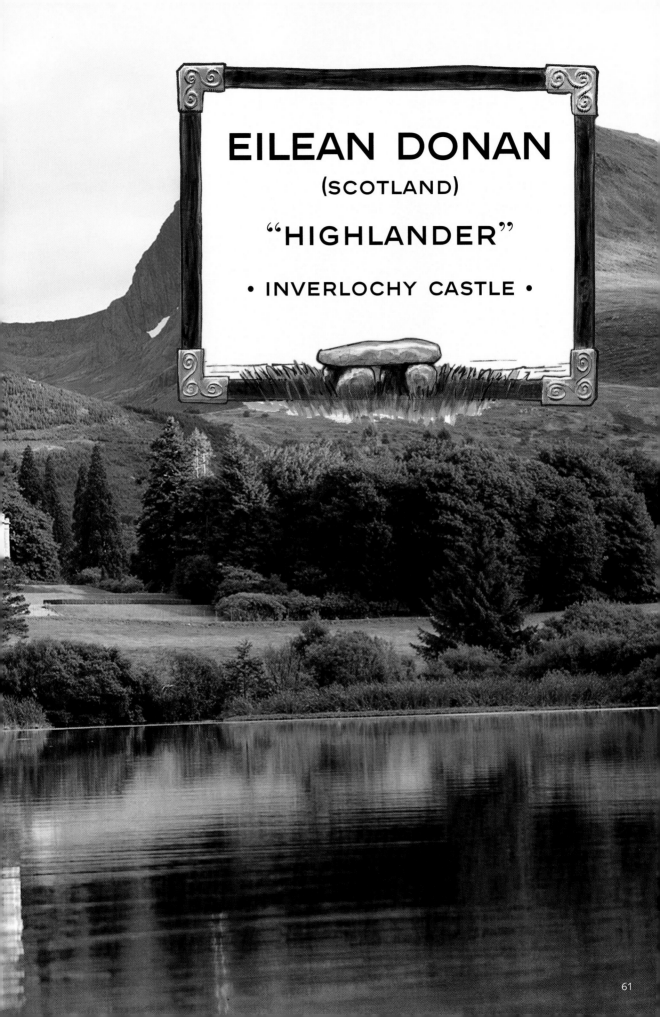

EILEAN DONAN

(SCOTLAND)

"HIGHLANDER"

· INVERLOCHY CASTLE ·

Banquet room in Eilean Donan castle.

"Eilean Donan" means Donan Island, and when you see this incredible speck of land with its great castle looming on the shores of Loch Duich, you will immediately know this is what Scotland is really like: A historic jewel, a last invincible stronghold. A fantastic little marvel that is nearly linked, but not quite, to the rest of the world. Needless to say, Eilean Donan, named after an Irish saint, was the scene for millions of bloody battles. A fortress against the Vikings and a Jacobite stronghold, the castle was originally given to the Mackenzies for services rendered in battle. During the 14th Century, this bastion offered hospitality to the great Scottish hero Robert Bruce when he fled from the English and who devised many plots whilst there before becoming King. Another stirring tale describes the welcome given to guests: a row of heads belonging to villains exhibited on the ramparts to give them cause for joy! This was a sight to cheer up even the dour and unaccommodating Earl of Murray, half brother of the ill-fated Mary Queen of Scots. Devastated, bombed, left in ruins, the remains then entertained the ghost of a Spanish soldier killed during the destruction of the castle in 1719 who, according to legend, still walks around with his head under his arm. This fabulous fortress has now been faithfully restored in accordance with an eerie vision seen by Farquhar MacRae, a dream later confirmed by old plans

that were unearthed well after the work was completed. Truly, Russell Mulcahy could not have found a better setting for his film *Highlander*. The scenario begins in the Scottish Highlands in 1518, and chronicles the adventures of Conner McLeod (Christopher Lambert) who, after being killed during a battle, becomes immortal, taking him through a thousand times and places to meet another immortal being, played by authentic Scotsman Sir Sean Connery. Everybody on Eilean Donan remembers the shooting very well. Pamela MacRea, the charming tour organizer, recalls how excited everyone in the whole area was and Robina MacGregor, the sympathetic guide,

Highlander leaving to the sound of "Long Live MacLeod".

recalls the ads put up in shops inviting men to let both their beards and hair grow out. She can still remember the mock Scottish village that took only a few days to build on the shore opposite the island, with the sun shining brilliantly throughout the month of May. Unheard of in Scotland, but the film director very quickly remedied the situation by projecting fake fog from a boat. Robina can still recall all the children playing in the little village. The people in the area, who came for the casting remember the weight of the costumes. Memories make everyone smile, but particularly those who took part in the film and who appear in the photos exhibited in the welcome center. Dunvegan, the fabulous dwelling of the McLeod clan who are still its proud owners, is not far from Eilean Donan, on the Isle of Skye. A trio of Scottish ladies, with a fine sense of humor, is in charge of entrance to both the castle and the superb park. The rooms are filled with memories from family photos that depict famous bagpipe players and old portraits that are stirring for such a remote part of this other quite amazing isle that is home to sheep and fresh peat, to mountains that are simply out of this world, to the Cuillins of Skye so revered by alpinists, to waterfalls, to glaciers, to isles, to cliffs and to a tiny bay with colorful cottages that is

Eilean Donan on Loch Duich.

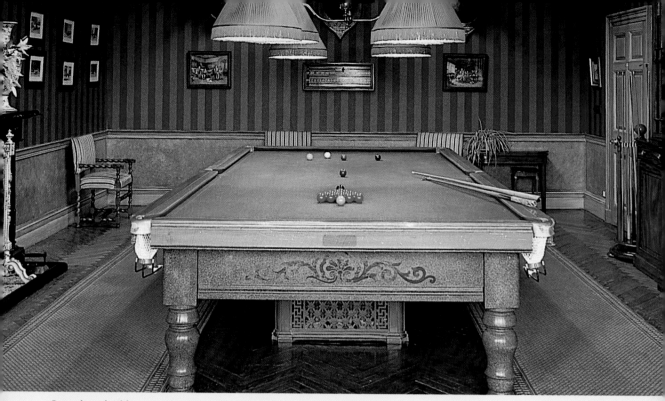

Preceding double pages: *Sean Connery and Christophe Lambert in "Highlander".*
Above: *The period billiard room and bedrooms....All that Scottish atmosphere.*

part of the view from the Cuillins Hills Hotel.

To the south, beyond Eilean Donan, amongst scenery so stunning that you are forced to stop and stare in awe, another national wonder awaits: Inverlochy Castle, one of the most magnificent hotels in the United Kingdom located at the foot of the famous Ben Nevis peak, the highest in Great Britain, where you can even go skiing! On the shore of its own loch in a fabulous setting of glens where quite incredible shades of russet, green and mauve are displayed in autumn, since 1863 Inverlochy Castle has received guests, monarchs and celebrities (including Christopher Lambert and Sean Connery who, as a fervent nationalist, is always amenable to wearing a kilt). The luxury is discreet, delicately subtle, and warm because it is so natural. Beautiful magazines and a variety of objects that give life to the room have been left everywhere

around the superb salon. Hikers leave their walking boots by the chimney where a large fire burns continuously. Small details in the beautiful bedrooms create the feeling of being entertained as a close, intimate friend: used paperbacks, a bottle of water put at your disposal, videos of movies shot in the area are piled up on a table in the billiard room, and with fishing rods and nets just asking to be used are in the entrance hall. All these special touches make Inverlochy Castle quite unique and are the reasons for being included in the very elegant *Condé Nast Traveler* magazine's Gold List. You can also go hunting for that famous grouse of course, play golf, walk in the wonderful landscaped park, read *Macbeth* whilst ensconced in a large armchair in the Drawing Room, or visit the legendary Ben Nevis distillery created by Long John MacDonald, aptly named because he was apparently over two meters

tall. His nickname went all the way round the world on labels of the famous "Long John" blend. Then there is also the charming little grocery store Peter MacLennan & Co. created in 1860 in Fort William that sells marmalade, chutney and all sorts of shortbread, as well as kilts and all the necessary accessories to accompany them in the adjoining shop and their very Scottish website: www.peter-maclennan.co.uk.

We owe electric light, color photography, the thermos flask, telephones, bicycles and golf clubs to Scotland. We are also indebted to Scotland for the scenery that can only be found there: Dramatically stunning, raw and rugged, fiendishly extravagant, peopled with headless riders and lakeside monsters, separated from the rest of the world, and yes, quite separate.

INVERLOCHY CASTLE
TORLUNDY
FORT WILLIAM PH33 6SN
UNITED KINGDOM
RELAIS & CHÂTEAUX
TEL.: + 44 (13) 97 70 81 77
FAX: + 44 (13) 97 70 29 53
info@inverlochy.co.uk
www.inverlochycastlehotel.co.uk

17 rooms from $322 to $692
(during off-peak season),
and from $456 to $865
(during peak season).
Table d'hôte, tennis court, golf course,
billiard room, fishing and pigeon shooting…

How to get there
From Glasgow, you only need
allow 2 hours by car: take the A82
highway to Fort Williams.
Inverlochy is 4 km to the north
of Fort Williams (A82).
To reach Eilean Donan,
drive for 1½ hours on
the road to Skye (A87).

HIVA OA
(MARQUESAS ISLANDS)

JACQUES BREL

• HIVA OA HANAKEE
PEARL LODGE •

As Jacques Brel sings: "Time stands still... in the Marquesas Islands."

A fascination for these islands can occur at any time and in the most unexpected people. It only takes one visit, one sudden overwhelming feeling of extraordinary peace. *You Will Tell Them*, the book written by Jacques Brel's last companion, Maddly Bamy, is a testimony to this. It is difficult to imagine the usually solemn-looking Belgian singer in a flower patterned shirt in the tropics.

Yet, because of his fascination with flying (he trained as a pilot and having finally obtained his license after many attempts) he flew over the islands in 1977 in his *Twin Bonanza*, a twin engine aircraft, named "Jojo" after his lifelong friend. He was in fact an adventurer; an eccentric but also a rebel, and who was never where he was expected to be. Actor, singer, composer, interpreter,

navigator, pilot, unpredictable, and erratic, he dreamt of bringing alive the spirit of those early days in the history of aviation, the challenges of the French airmail service. Frenetic tours, one show following after another, recitals in succession at the Olympia in Paris, the Royal Albert Hall in London, Carnegie Hall, then Russia, Finland and everywhere else. He wanted to find another life and finally discovered the happiness he sought in the Marquesas Islands. Indeed, he could not have found a better place than in these islands. At the time, as Maddly tells us, the journey from Papeete to the Marquesas Islands, or from the Marquesas Islands back to Papeete, sometimes took months, as each island was only allocated three seats on a flight per week. The island that appealed to him the

Above: *The bungalows at Hiva Oa Hanakee Pearl Lodge.*
Opposite: *Jacques Brel on his boat, the "Askoy II".*

most was Hiva Oa. He discovered it in 1975 with his wife after fifty-nine days of navigation in the Pacific Ocean on board his yacht *Askoy*. He chose it quite simply because it was the place where he immediately felt at ease. "I have finally found some peace here", he said.

He was passionately fond of the Marquesas Islands. He forgot his illness there, was overflowing with energy, proudly growing his own fruit and vegetables, leading the life that had always attracted him: a rather basic existence where everyone had to fend for himself. At one time, prior to discovering the islands, he had even thought quite seriously about setting up a business in chicken farming. He finally achieved this separation with his former way of life through this new adventure and was thus prevented from becoming like the people he detested, who would not move and were prudent. "There are many things that you cannot find on the island, but", as he said again, "these things serve no purpose". No television, no electricity, but only oil which did just as well. He read poetry and novels including *The Island* by Robert Merle, one of his favorite books, talked a lot, laughed even more, received important news via the Papeete broadcasting station transmitter. A message

a few minutes long was more than enough. "Enough to know whether there is a war or not". Friends, locals, as well as other pilots, often stopped off to say hello, bringing with them iceboxes filled with fresh produce for him. This was all he needed. This was where he wrote the song "Les Marquises" shortly after his arrival there. The song tells of tropical nights, fearsome sun, coconut trees, lascivious women, non-existent winters, and of time that stands still. The album immediately sold without any advertising and, more or less as soon as the record was launched, the singer returned to Hiva Oa. He died there in 1978, and was buried in the little cemetery of Atuona, a few yards from the burial place of Paul Gauguin.

Puamau beach, on the east coast of Hiva Oa.

Today, regular flights connect Hiva Oa with Papeete, but the island has remained just as it was when Jacques Brel fell in love with it. It still gives the impression of being remote, isolated, unknown, wild, and tailor-made for adventurers. The inhabitants of the Marquesas Islands are French, but legends still form a major part of their lives. Legends of their tribe, their land, their huts, their places of worship, of nature, and simple values that are dear to them. Legends of the magical powers of the elders, of sacred sites, of a completely different way of life where every word conjures up visions of power and mystery. Prior to developing a more conventional way of exprising themselves in writing, they nevertheless perfected a method by way of tattoos that still remains today, and is famous all over the world. All of these customs are part of life at Hiva Oa and are used in many ways.

The Hiva Oa Hanakee Pearl Lodge for example, which dominates the Bay of Tahauku opposite the majestic Mount Temetiu, required twenty sculptors to decorate the bedrooms. The result combines sculptured wood, stone and local materials, and is a credit to Oceanic Art. The bungalows and family suites look out over the ocean, Tahauku Bay, and Tehueto Valley. You can visit the village where La Maison du Jouir can be found (a faithful reconstruction of Gauguin's house) either on foot, bicycle or by Land Rover. The Island's valleys, with a wealth of archaeological sites, are also easily accessible. The hotel offers a restaurant, a shop, five bungalows with a superb view of the mountain and nine others overlooking the ocean, a swimming pool around which candlelight dinners are served. A small welcoming resort that is perfect for travelers dreaming of adventure. Here you may live to the

relaxed rhythm of the Marquesas Islands, taking time to be quiet, to listen, to see, to admire. The hotel organizes excursions in all-purpose vehicles, walks in the valleys, horseback-riding through banana trees and paw paw groves, and days out on boats. Everything is easy, magnificent, and laid-back. Since time immemorial, bays, majestic waterfalls, silent under woods, volcanic mountains that appear untouched by mankind have always attracted artists and writers, including Herman Melville, Pierre Loti, Robert Louis Stevenson, Jack London.

The Marquesas Islands owe their name to the Spanish navigator Alvaro de Mendana who called them Islas Marquesas de Mendoza in honor of the Vice King of Peru's wife. The islands remain one of the wildest places in the world. A far-away mysterious territory to the northeast of Tahiti that intrigues and makes you dream, without really knowing why. "Jojo", Jacques Brel's little Bonanza, is on display near the aircraft runway. Both memories and emotions are very much at home in the Marquesas Islands.

HIVA OA HANAKEE PEARL LODGE
PO BOX 80
ATUONA
MARQUESAS ISLANDS
TEL.: + 689 927 587
FAX: + 689 927 595
hiva.oa.pearl@mail.pf
www.pearlresorts.com

20 bungalows from $209 to $333.
Restaurant, bar, horse riding, excursions by land rover to discover the wealth of the Islands…

How to get there
From the Papeete international airport,
a 3-hour flight will take you to Atuona airport,
only 20 minutes from the hotel.

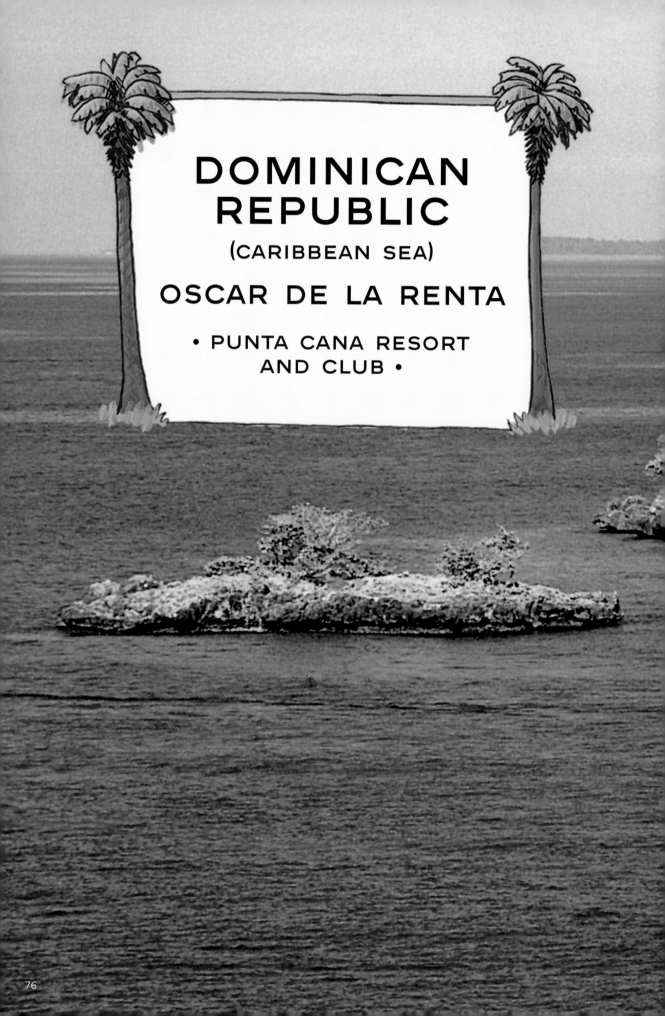

DOMINICAN REPUBLIC

(CARIBBEAN SEA)

OSCAR DE LA RENTA

• PUNTA CANA RESORT
AND CLUB •

One of the villas at the Punta Cana Resort and Club.

"I remember the colors, the flowers, the sun. Wherever I go, I cannot bear to be far from the sun. Sunrise will remain something magical for me. When I was a child we had a house just one street away from the sea front, in the center of the old part of Santo Domingo, the most ancient of old towns in this hemisphere, the capital of the first island colonized by Christopher Columbus in 1492. We are proud of this. All my mother's family lived in the same district. An enclosed life, intimate and protected". Oscar de la Renta's first memories of Santo Domingo in the Thirties make you thirsty to discover more about this island. He continues: "We also had a yard at the back of the house that my mother divided into plots where each child could do as he liked. I planted corn and spinach that grew at the most amazing speed and sold them to my mother". He remembers the enormous mango tree in the garden, the hibiscus, polyantha, and ylang-ylang in the square whose flowers dispensed their aroma over the whole district. "Every time I smell this scent, I feel as if I am back there". He did not forget the scent when he created his first fragrance. As you listen to his descriptions, you can imagine traveling with him along old streets lined with houses painted in pastel shades or just sitting with him there, next to his uncle's friend, a Russian beauty called Elena who told him travel stories. You can imagine the island as it was then, far away, unheard of, overrun by cane sugar and tobacco. You can feel the heavy atmosphere of a Catholic country, the political conflicts as well as the exuberance, tenderness, and joy of living in a house that was always bursting with people, where parents, grandparents, uncles, aunts, nephews, nieces and friends all crossed each other's paths. You can imagine the sunrise, smell, music, and atmosphere..., Madrid, New York, a career that created his international fame. De la Renta's enthusiasm is exceptional: not only for fashion, but for the world of travel, as well. For example, on his first trip to Andalusia, traveling alongside peasants setting off for the olive harvest, he traveled third class with a book of tickets "that entitled me to journey 4,800 kilometeres by train". Nowadays Oscar de la Renta returns to Santo Domingo whenever he has the chance, or rather to the Dominican Republic, as this part of the island is called

Oscar de la Renta at home, in Casa de Campo.

The golf course designed by Paul Burke Dye.

since its separation from Haiti. The island that Christopher Columbus named Hispaniola and where the first cathedrals, the first hospitals, the first streets, and the first schools in the New World were built, is reputedly home to the most beautiful colonial district in Latin America, amongst other treasures. Once again, Oscar de la Renta found there that kindness, that spontaneity, that frater-

nity, that well-known, laid-back-island-feeling, which together sum up the very essence of the Latin American soul. "There is something very different in Latin America in comparison to other parts of the world. When I walk down the streets, sometimes a Venezuelan or an Equatorial man recognizes me and says: "O, Mr. de la Renta, we are so proud of you, you are one of us! Have

The Punta Cana Resort and Club.

you ever heard an Italian say to a French man, 'I am so pleased that you are European like myself! We feel a certain closeness between us, as if we were one".

His impact has been considerable with the Dominican people. From the few words exchanged, you can really sense the admiration and respect. Some talk of his huma-nitarian work, of Casa del Nino that he created with his wife, Annette, in order to take care of 1,200 hundred children who attend school everyday, and come to the daytime dispensary or the daycare for newborn babies that allows their mothers to go out to work. Punta Cana is also one of the most famous places in the island, because he has helped considerably in making it so well-known.

One of his projects has resulted in an association with the Dominican entrepreneur Frank Rainieri and the New York lawyer Theodore Kheel, both pioneers of tourism in the region. During the Sixties, the duo developed this incredible estate on the south coast of the island. Nowadays this exclusive resort entertains visitors from all over the world. The Punta Cana Resort and Club, whose decor was conceived by Oscar de la Renta, is one of the most beautiful hotels in the Dominican Republic. A never-ending white sand beach borders the turquoise blue waters of the Caribbean Sea. The resort is home to the famous Paul Burke Dye- designed golf course, an archery field and an international marina. There are a plethora of activities, including horses that are always ready for riding. The resort's private nature reserve, the Punta Cana Ecological Park, offers daily tours to guests along trails that meander through a tropical paradise of plants, animals and thousands of butterflies, a kingdom of lush

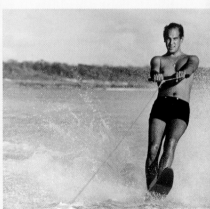

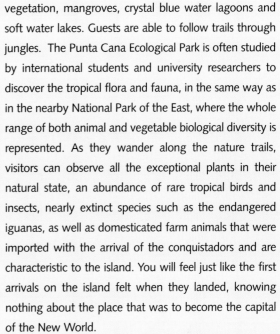

vegetation, mangroves, crystal blue water lagoons and soft water lakes. Guests are able to follow trails through jungles. The Punta Cana Ecological Park is often studied by international students and university researchers to discover the tropical flora and fauna, in the same way as in the nearby National Park of the East, where the whole range of both animal and vegetable biological diversity is represented. As they wander along the nature trails, visitors can observe all the exceptional plants in their natural state, an abundance of rare tropical birds and insects, nearly extinct species such as the endangered iguanas, as well as domesticated farm animals that were imported with the arrival of the conquistadors and are characteristic to the island. You will feel just like the first arrivals on the island felt when they landed, knowing nothing about the place that was to become the capital of the New World.

PUNTA CANA RESORT AND CLUB
PUNTA CANA BEACH
HIGUEY
DOMINICAN REPUBLIC
TEL.: + 809 221 2262
FAX: + 809 688 3951
reservas@puntacana.com
www.puntacana.com

Rooms and suites from $80 to $195,
Beach villas from $350 to $650,
Gold villas from $450 to $1,950.
5 restaurants and 5 bars, live concerts
and La Proa night club, excursions to
Punta Cana Ecological Foundation nature reserve,
sea side golf course, private marina,
beauty salon, around the clock medical
assistance, business center…

How to get there
From Punta Cana international airport,
a cab will take you to the hotel in 10 minutes.

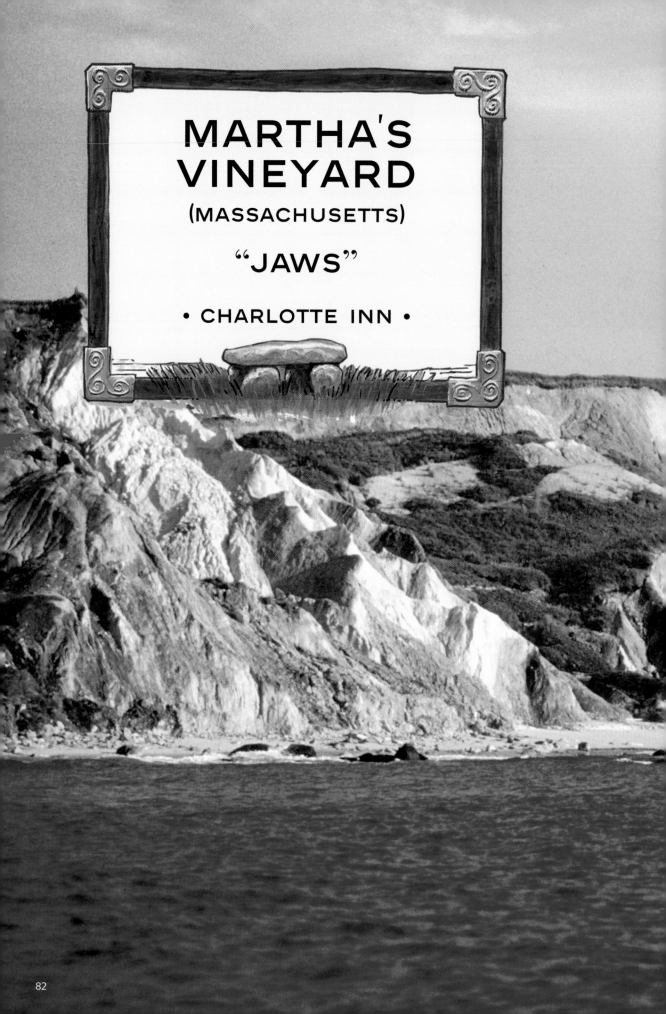

MARTHA'S VINEYARD
(MASSACHUSETTS)

"JAWS"

• CHARLOTTE INN •

Robert Shaw, Roy Scheider and Richard Dreyfuss.

Los Angeles 1974 – Steven Spielberg, twenty-six years old, was in Richard Zanuck's office (his producer and friend), when he saw the manuscript of an unpublished book, the story of a shark, "an airplane book" according to Spielberg, who read it effortlessly. The author was a former Washington Post and Newsweek journalist Peter Benchley. The studio had bought the rights for $175,000 but did not know how to develop them. Spielberg commented to his friend that he could do something with it and that it might be fun. "So they gave me the movie", said Spielberg. The story did not exist for the public and neither did the book. "We did everything we could to make it a best seller!" Spielberg and Zanuck went about it so well that the book was one of the best-selling books in California. The studio did not know what to do when they bought the rights, but Spielberg made it an international box office hit, the first blockbuster in the history of motion pictures, one of the most terrifying movies ever made and the first to break the symbolic barrier of $100 million, ending its run at $260 million.

The story takes us to Amity, a small seaside resort on the East Coast of the United States a few days before the tourist season is due to commence. The body of a young woman is found on the beach, atrociously mutilated. The chief of police believes the young girl to be the victim of a shark. The mayor, quite determined to make the most of the tourist season, does not want to hear anything about this. Roy Scheider, whom Spielberg had admired in *The French Connection*, plays the sheriff. Richard Dreyfuss, who had just finished *American Graffiti*, is the shark specialist. Robert Shaw, the theatre actor who had just finished *The Sting*, plays the part of the sailor who offers his boat to track down the monster. Spielberg wanted to shoot in the Hamptons, but eventually found this location too sophisticated. Joe Alves, the production designer, suggested Martha's Vineyard. The golden coastline, immaculate and unspoilt, the small port, the deserted beaches, the Victorian-style houses, the view that melts into the horizon, and the sandy depths were perfect for the equipment. Everything was ideal. In 1974 the team settled on the island from May to September and went

Poster detail of the movie.

Façade of Charlotte Inn.

out to sea every day to shoot from 7 in the morning to 7 at night. They also shot some footage in the small town of Edgartown, in Menemsha port on the Joseph Sylva State Beach. Robert Mattey, head of special effects for the Disney studios, created three mechanical sharks, each for different movements of the animal, mixed together for the scenes with live sharks, a real brain teaser. The models

did not work properly. The first sank immediately. The second exploded. The weather was bad and they had to wait for even the slightest rays of sun. From July onwards the island was invaded by holiday goers whose boats were forever getting in the way of the cameras and film crew. There were so many memories...

Since then Martha's Vineyard has recovered its peace and

Preceding double pages: *One of the island's most famous lighthouses and Menemsha harbor.*
Above: *Since the shooting of "Jaws", Martha's Vineyard has recovered its peace and quiet.*

quiet and no shark has ever been seen. In the Atlantic Ocean off Cape Cod, the Island was originally inhabited by the Wampanoag Indians, whose descendants still live to the south. The English navigator Bartholomew Gosnold then discovered it in 1602 and decided to link his daughter's name with the vines that grew wild there. A weekend and holiday getaway for the Kennedys, the Clintons, Carly Simon, Spike Lee, Sharon Stone and many others, Martha's Vineyard draws its charm from the New England atmosphere, chocolate box cottages, abrupt cliffs, magnificent beaches, a port always full of boats, and a thousand other refinements. A beautiful lighthouse, bicycles leaning against a flower-decked fence, a long wooden pier, and typical streets such as Lamberts Cove Road. In the lovely little town of Edgartown, "Amity" in the movie, you lose count of the number of neat little shops, art

galleries, restaurants and charming hotels such as Charlotte Inn at the heart of the village, one of the most delightful hotels in the United States. The main building, now surrounded by linden and chestnut trees, dates from 1864 and has welcomed guests since 1920. It is all about those little details, souvenirs, and things that tell of a life well-lived: The Edwardian architecture, manicured garden, antiques in every room, rocking chairs, hunting pictures, hats and coats hung deliberately on the antique stand. The fine staircase leads to the bedrooms and the cozy suites, decorated with silver and porcelain pieces, crystal lamps, period furniture, and vases bursting with colorful flowers. Not far from the main building are four other equally charming houses, renovated with the same flair, to receive faithful guests who return regularly. Each of the twenty-three rooms and two suites are intimate and

welcoming; each shettering a mini museum designed by an artistic and passionate soul. The very chic restaurant L'Etoile, famous all over the island for its French cuisine and delicious local produce, is never empty. In nice weather, guests may sit in the garden or on the pretty flowered terrace for dinner or cocktails by candlelight. Spend your days cycling, lounging on the beach, tuna fishing on one of the many charter boats. Play golf, visit Oak Bluffs, another delightful village a few miles from Edgartown, famous for its doll's houses called "gingerbread houses". Festivals, concerts, recitals, cruises to other islands like tiny Block Island, a magnificent nature reserve, kayak trips, historic walks, Thanksgiving celebrations and a barbecue on July 4th. Time flies by quickly it does at Charlotte Inn.

CHARLOTTE INN
27 SOUTH STREET
EDGARTOWN, MA 02539
USA
RELAIS & CHÂTEAUX
TEL.: + 1 (508) 627 4151
FAX: + 1 (508) 627 4652
charlotte@relaischateaux.com
www.relaischateaux.com/charlotte

23 rooms from $325 to $595,
and 2 suites from $450 to $895;
possible rental of 2 individual dwellings
(the Carriage House and the Coach House…).
L'Étoile restaurant and bar, kayak excursions,
islands tours, golf course only 6 kilometers away
*Attention: closed every year between
2nd January and 13th February.*

How to get there
From Boston, take Route 3 until Woods Hole,
then the ferry for Vineyard Haven.
There is also a daily flight between Boston
and Martha's Vineyard.

CORSICA
(FRANCE)

HENRI MATISSE

• LE MAQUIS •

Sun, color, light.

Matisse, a great traveler? Yes, Matisse was a great traveler. Morocco provided him of course with that complete change of scenery way beyond his wildest dreams, but there was also New York, Pittsburgh, San Francisco, Tahiti, Chicago, Los Angeles, Algeria, Majorca and Seville... Yet there was nothing bohemian about Matisse. He preferred a well-adjusted and regular lifestyle, the harmony of an ordinary existence. In 1898, he married Amélie Parayre and the young couple went on their honeymoon to London, where the artist saw the work of his colleague J.M.W. Turner. The couple then decided to visit Ajaccio where Amelia's sister was a schoolteacher. This trip was a determining factor for Matisse. He not only experienced boundless joy in painting outdoors, far from all academia and exhibitions, but he also discovered something that directly influenced his work: Mediterranean colors. "It was in Ajaccio", he later said, "that my great admiration of the south began". Later he added: "I spent a year in Corsica. By going to this amazing country, I was able to get to know the Mediterranean. I was dazzled. Everything shines there, everything is in color, everything is light". This first trip inspired him with several studies and paintings such as *Corsican Scenery: The Pink Wall* (the wall of Ajaccio hospital) and *The Courtyard of the Mill in Ajaccio.*

After meeting up with Matisse again after this trip, his friend, the Belgian artist Evenepoël, wrote to his father, "I saw Matisse on his return from Corsica. He brought back some extraordinary studies painted by a mad epileptic impressionist! I told him what I thought. It is quite nonsensical. Particularly for someone who had such satisfying artistic qualities". Other artists followed the example shown by Matisse: Fernand Léger, James Whistler, Maurice Utrillo, Suzanne Valadon and Paul Signac.

Sun, color and light were the three elements he always aspired towards during his journeys to Collioure, St. Tropez, Tahiti, and in his Nice workshop surrounded by his white pigeons. As he said himself, he was forever seeking other areas and other proportions. Travel aided him in his

View from one of the rooms in Le Maquis as if it were a painting.

92

Photograph of Matisse by Henri Cartier-Bresson in 1951.

quest. His trips provided him with an opportunity to take a step back and have a different perception of things, as well as a certain freedom. "When you have worked for a long time in the same place", he said, "it is beneficial to stop at some point. When you travel, the brain works in a different way. Some parts are rested but so many others are allowed to come forth". His life in Nice and in Vence, where he created the superb Rosary Chapel, a stained glass window that is quite unique, portrays this continual quest for sun, light and a certain freedom.

There is no doubt that Corsica will continue to inspire artists. The smell of Corsica is a powerful stimulus. As soon as the aircraft doors open even a fraction, the smell of the Corsican scrub invades the air: Honey, wild flowers, pine

Le Maquis hotel's exotic garden.

trees, chestnuts, heather, "ciste" trees with their sticky resin, myrtles with their black berries, fruit trees laden with red fruit, olive trees, green oaks. It is impossible to count them. This never-to-be-forgotten smell can only be found in Corsica. Even whilst traveling along the road to Ajaccio, you already feel isolated from the rest of civilization. The town where Napoleon was born blends all the charm of the French Riviera with that of Italy, with its typical ochre walls, its port with traditional boats, elegant palm trees, market displaying donkey sausages, chestnut polenta, fig jam, almond "canistrelli", honey nougat, myrtle and cedar alcohol. For 500 years, the island was Genoese. It became French in 1768, a few months before Napoleon was born. Everything about the place expresses this combination. The language, the customs, the scenery.

In Le Maquis hotel, less than ten minutes from Ajaccio, all those wonderful Corsican traditions have been kept and sublimated. Ketty Salini, the dynamic owner, started out by opening a bistro in Porticcio. As a young woman, she had always dreamt of establishing the most beautiful hotel on the island and as soon as she was able, she spent a night at The Ritz in Paris "to understand how it all worked". Today her four-star luxury hotel is a place that dreams are made of, as discovered by anyone who is lucky enough to stay there. This magnificent property, in a waterfront setting over the Bay of Ajaccio, has all the elegance of a family house. Period engravings stylishly adorn one of the walls, charming drawings and traditional objects are chosen with great care. The refined rooms so nice, with that wonderful aroma of wax about them. The garden, with its beautiful stone steps, assembles all varieties of plants and flowers, mimosas, eucalyptus,

lavenders, and parasol pine trees. You will stroll around as in a dream, with your face uplifted, a little stunned by something so exotic yet so close to the chaos of Paris. From the hotel it is very easy to walk to the mountain villages, to follow the small paths interspersed with rivers and pretty streams, to discover the picturesque pathways amidst beech and chestnut trees. Stop off at the typically Corsican restaurant Auberge du Prunelli in the valley of the same name, near a pretty little river. All the walks are as surprising as they are enchan-ting, and the hotel reception will be pleased to share details of the most scenic routes. From the hotel terrace your delighted eyes can greedily lap up the magnificent panorama of moun-tainous landscape, contrasted with the cool calm of the beach, and sea that stretches as far as the Sanguinary islands. Sun, color, light...

LE MAQUIS
B.P. 94
20166 PORTICCIO (CORSICA)
FRANCE
SMALL LEADING HOTELS OF THE WORLD
TEL.: + 33 (4) 95 25 05 55
FAX: + 33 (4) 95 25 11 70
info@lemaquis.com
www.lemaquis.com

22 rooms from $151 to $259 (off-peak season),
and from $324 to $486 (peak season);
5 suites from $227 to $594 (off-peak season),
and from $486 to $973 (peak season).
L'Arbousier restaurant, bar, 2 swimming pools,
thalassotherapy, tennis court, nautical sports,
golf course, riding…

How to get there
Ajaccio airport is 20 minutes from the hotel. By car,
take the A road 196 in the direction of Bonifacio,
then follow the sign for Porticcio (C.D. 55).

SEYCHELLES
(INDIAN OCEAN)

"GOODBYE, EMMANUELLE"

• FREGATE ISLAND PRIVATE •

Fregate Island Private.

Sometimes all it takes is just one photo and an exotic dream becomes reality: A scantily-dressed young woman sitting languorously in a wicker armchair. It seems like only yesterday that the film director, Just Jaeckin, introduced sexual freedom by allowing the world to discover a young Dutch model, Sylvia Kristel. His *Emmanuelle*, the first and only film he directed himself, based on Emmanuelle Arsan's erotic novel, had a phenomenal success and rapidly became a cult film. Everyone desperately wanted to see the film with such a scandalous reputation. It was impossible to count the Japanese coaches that stopped in front of the triumphant UGC cinema on the Champs-Elysées in Paris, where *Emmanuelle* ran for ten years. In the States, it was X-rated and a watered-down version was distributed. It turned out to be the biggest French hit in the American box office. Sylvia Kristel's sensuality, Pierre Bachelet's memorable song, Thailand and those interminable beaches and the idyllic scenery had already become permanently associated with the film. In 1978, *Goodbye Emmanuelle*, directed this time by François Leterrier, showed the world yet more magical scenery, that of a heavenly island lost in the Indian Ocean to the north of Madagascar and hitherto unknown, La Digue. Emmanuelle led an ideal, free lifestyle in the Seychelles.

Nevertheless, her happiness was overshadowed when she discovered that her friend, Clara, could no longer bear this existence. A young film director turned up, Gregory was looking for a house in which to shoot a film. To the tune of Serge Gainsbourg's sensual song, a colonial house built of palm tree leaves and wood appears, surrounded by wild and sheltered nature...

Today the house belongs to President René who has entertained Tony Blair, among others. Reproduced on a bank note and part of the Union Estate, a national park at the end of the South Road, where patchouli, saffron and vanilla plants still stand. After going through a small portal, visitors wander amongst coconut trees and giant turtles before peacefully continuing in the direction of the "Treasure Cove", one of the fabulous sites in the Seychelles, with its rocks sculptured by erosion tumbling

"Goodbye, Emmanuelle."

Poster of the legendary movie featuring Sylvia Kristel.

right down to the sandy white beach. The only way to travel here is by bike or ox cart along earthen tracks where the air is heavy with the fragrance of hibiscus, sandalwood or ylang ylang. You can imagine the amazement of Arab navigators, who were the first to discover the Seychelles in the 9th Century. Then in 1502 the Portuguese came and used the islands as a port of call on their way to the Indies, followed by pirates, who apparently left undiscovered treasures there. In the 18th Century, French settlers took possession of these unin-

habited islands, and then the British officially took over until their independence in 1976. La Digue is only one of the 115 islands in this magnificent territory. Nearby is Mahé, the main island, and the one that the visitors first discover when their aircraft lands. The market here is overflowing with spices and local produce, as well as impressive sharks' jaws. Then there is Praslin, the exquisitely beautiful Vallée de Mai, Adam and Eve's earthly paradise according to the legend, and a fitting setting for the famous "Coco de Mer" palm tree, whose fruit,

A paradise barely three square kilometers in size.

shaped like a female pelvis, has been nicknamed "Coco Fesses" because of their extremely suggestive shape. A national treasure that you can only acquire in La Digue or Praslin with a ministerial certificate! Moreover, the valley has become a UNESCO heritage site and you can only visit it by following specific paths so as not to bother animals or disturb certain plants whilst they are flowering or bearing fruit.

A little further on, at about twenty minutes from Mahé, is Frégate, a tiny private hideaway (3.2 km), also very much appreciated by pirates in bygone days. Coconut, paw paw and mandarin trees, filaos, shadowy pathways that criss-cross the whole island, giant turtles and millions of birds, frigates set up home in the midst of a luxuriant and colorful vegetation. You only have to lift up your eyes to discover rare species of trees and plants, astonishing

and curious animals. This is where Fregate Island Private was created. Sixteen superb villas with woven palm tree roofs, sophisticated to the extreme, emerge quite naturally from the vegetation. Teak and acajou rooms are delicately refined, with antiques from Bali, Malaysia and Thailand. Large private terraces looking over the ocean give an impression of living outdoors. Air remains mild all year round. A soft water swimming pool is hewn from the rock, deep-sea fishing boats, yachts, sailing boats, bicycles are available for rent and to ride all over the tiny island paths, diving sessions, walking tours, as well as visiting the other islands are always available. Everything has been laid on to make life sweet and beautiful. The hotel botanist enthusiastically shows you wild life that is particularly protected here. Moreover, the hotel logo is in honor of the birds that gave their name to the island.

The elegant frigates that, along with the other species living on the island, make rare bird lovers very happy. For the more melancholy, the library and beaches surrounded by the most astonishing blocks of pink granite offer all the peace and quiet you could possibly ever dream of. The exotic dream has remained untouched since *Goodbye, Emmanuelle*. After all, as Henri de Monfreid, the famous French novelist wrote, "The Seychelles Islands were made for love. The only things born here are children".

FREGATE ISLAND PRIVATE
PO BOX 330 VICTORIA
MAHÉ
REPUBLIC OF SEYCHELLES
TEL.: + 248 324 545
FAX: + 248 324 499
fregate@seychelles.net
www.fregate.com

16 villas with private solarium and Jacuzzi (minimum stay of 5 days), at $1,700 during off-peak season and $2,000 during peak season. Fregate House restaurant, Plantation House restaurant-bar, organic vegetable garden, fresh water swimming pool, fitness centre, large library and video library, tennis court, private port, diving centre, yacht and catamaran trips…

How to get there

Upon your arrival in Mahé, a helicopter or Air Seychelles charter (4 direct flights every week) will take you to Fregate in 20 minutes.

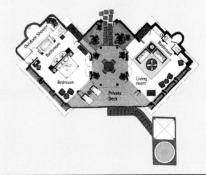

VANUA LEVU

(FIJI ISLANDS)

JEAN-MICHEL COUSTEAU

• FIJI ISLANDS RESORT •

One of the 25 "bures" in Jean-Michel Cousteau's Fiji Islands Resort.

Jean-Michel Cousteau's life could not have been any different. At the age of seven, he was "thrown" overboard by his father, fitted with an aqualung that "Le Commandant" had just perfected. Later on, he listened to all the enthusiastic discussions between his father and his father's friends on an innovative piece of equipment, a revolutionary camera, or a new mask model. At fifteen, he aspired towards becoming an architect to build houses under the sea, but as soon as he got his diploma, his destiny caught up with him and he rejoined his father aboard the legendary *Calypso*. The years passed by, mostly spent under water, one day leading him to starting up his own company to ensure, in association with Microsoft Corporation, the first link between an underwater diver and armchair surfers asking questions online. He founded a maritime research center in Marseilles, which led to him representing the US Pavilion at the Universal Exhibition in Lisbon. His company, the Ocean Futures Society, produced educational programs, led research and in 2002 at Salt Lake City, he was the first to represent the environment at the opening ceremony of the Olympic Games. For over forty years, Jean-Michel Cousteau devoted his life to the ocean, thus following in the footsteps of the work of the "man in the red bonnet". One day his travels led him to the area between Polynesia and

Australia in the Fiji archipelago, an exceptional location for divers all over the world. Several trips ensued, resulting in an attachment with these islands and their people, as well as the inspiration for a new project. In 1998, he linked his name with an American company that had recently renovated a hotel on Vanua Levu, one of the main islands, with the aim of transforming it into a family holiday venue that respected both local culture and the environment. It was called the "Jean-Michel Cousteau Fiji Island Resort". The idea was very simple: to draw close to nature and come alongside Fiji civilization by providing activities that are easy for everyone to do, such as guided tours accom-

Jean-Michel Cousteau.

Jetty at the foot of each "bure".

panied by biologists, forest excursions to discover, amongst other things, medicinal plants, and excursions to local villages to meet people. Always with the same preoccupations: for the appreciation, knowledge and conservation of an exceptional ecological environment and to prove that tourism and nature conservation can be reconciled. There is neither telephone nor television here. Just typical bungalows by the sea, "bures" where all the comforts one could possibly wish for are provided.

Civilization, including a shop, restaurant, bar, telephone and television, can be located nearby in the main building. A cheerful assortment of Indian, Fijian and European cuisine can be found on the restaurant menu. This is because all those who have settled on one or other of these 330 islands at some point in time have left behind their own traditions and customs. Combinations of Indians, Chinese, the British, a succession of missionaries, sailors from all walks of life, and escaping Australian

Preceding double pages: *"Captain Planet" during one of his expeditions.*
Above: *The swimming pool at the Fiji Islands Resort.*

prisoners have never ceased to provide Fiji with their specific attractions.

Divers of course have the advantage of quite a spectacular environment here. In Fiji, there are over 400 species of corals and over thirty sorts of butterfly fish, dolphins, skates, pilot whales, turtles, and a thousand other wonders. Thanks to "The Jean-Michel Cousteau Adventure", the diving center adjoining the vacation site, it is possible to approach them. There are around fifteen locations in the program, such as the one near the island of Namenalala. This is the furthest away, at about an hour's distance by boat, but is also considered as one of the most beautiful. Biology lovers can share their enthusiasm with a well-known biologist. For those who wish, every day offers a variety of boat trips or a "walk with a difference". One morning you may wish to go diving in the vicinity of

the coral reefs, equipped with a snorkel and mask and accompanied by a marine biologist. The next day there might be a hike into the tropical forest to admire the waterfalls or go for a swim. The next day, a guided tour might be planned into the mangrove with an explanation of the tropical ecosystem. Activities have also been organized for children who have their own center, the Bula Camp. Monitors greet them on arrival and each of them is given a member's card, the Bula Camp Passport, that opens the door to nine different adventures: a forest hike, meeting the inhabitants of a village, discovering coral reefs, to name a few. Completion of each expedition is indicated on a card that is stamped accordingly; this enables children to remember what was achieved. An amusing souvenir that might make them think perhaps, when they are about to throw a piece of paper on the

ground upon returning home. Parents can either share their activities or meet with them at the end of the day for an outdoor game of bingo, an explanation of life in the stars, a film, or a story told just as if it was in a book, for-ever disco-vering and learning nearly without realizing it. *Calypso* and "Captain Planet", as the most famous Frenchman in the world and his boat is nicknamed, have dropped anchor off all the islands you can possibly think of, Cap Vert, Caribbean, Bahamas, Alaska, Malta, Gozo, Catalina, Mariannes, Pomègues, etc. Their adventures make both adults and children dream, as well as those for whom our earth remains an extraordinarily curious and bewitching place. With Jean-Michel Cousteau, real adventure lives on.

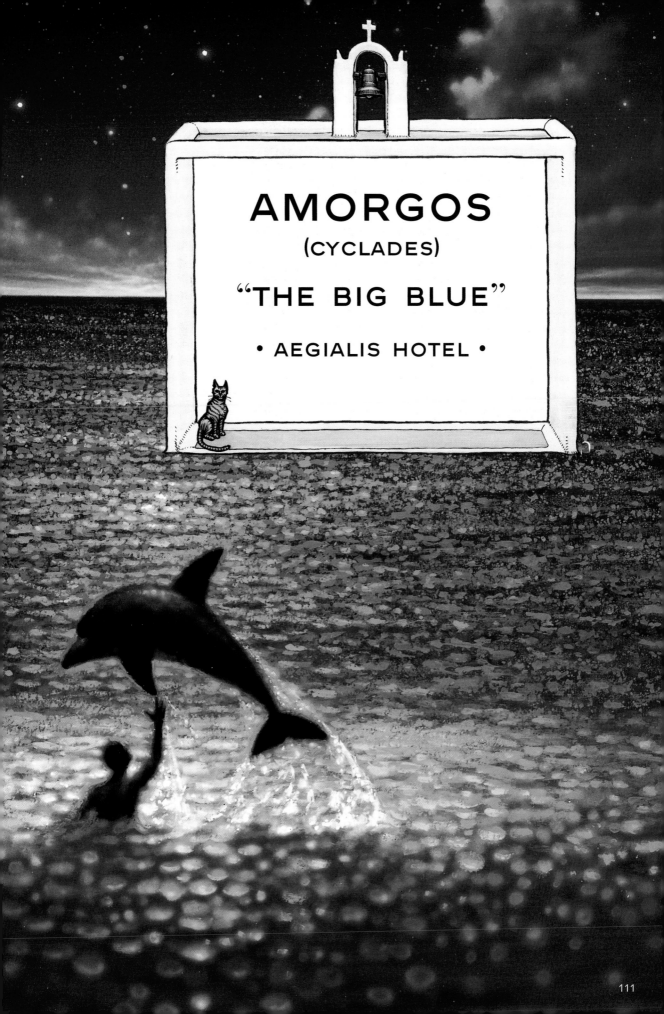

AMORGOS
(CYCLADES)

"THE BIG BLUE"

• AEGIALIS HOTEL •

Amorgos on the Aegean Sea.

A Greek island in black and white. Shots of the sun exploding over the stone. A child going to fetch his mask and flippers, hidden in the hollow of a rock. He remains motionless with his equipment in one hand, his eyes fixed intensely on the immense stretch of sea sprawled below...*The Big Blue*.

At the age of seventeen, Luc Besson was a scuba instructor, just like his parents. One evening, he saw the screening of footage for a film, in which a perfect stranger appeared, euphorically free diving towards the bottom of the ocean, to the unbelievable depth of 92 meters without oxygen. Jacques Mayol, the crazy world champion free diver was nicknamed "the dolphin man". The hero of *The Big Blue* had been discovered. Luc Besson spent his childhood at Ios near Amorgos, in the Aegian Sea. He wanted to recapture this atmosphere. His childhood memories and the scenario of the film complemented one other superbly. After direc-ting *The Last Battle*, he set out for Greece, to Ios then Amorgos. He felt the same atmosphere in Amorgos as he had experienced as a child. Then someone told him about a monastery that he just had to go and see. He went there and was overwhelmed at first sight. "I don't know when, I don't know where, but this monastery will be in *The Big Blue*". It was indeed in the film, from the very first black and white opening shots,

rugged, natural, laid bare, abstract, just like Greece. You could feel the heat burning rough surface of the rocks. The cool freshness of the water and the tranquil peace.

Color suddenly appeared, but everything else was already there, it was followed by the tale of two childhood friends who lived on the same Greek island, who had been separated but met up again for an ultimate and terribly tragic diving competition. Jean Reno was Enzo Molinari, the exuberant Italian, male chauvinist, and nervous show-off. Jean-Marc Barr played Jacques Mayol, the reserved Frenchman, timid and absent minded. Rosanna Arquette played the part of Johana, the pretty American girl whose destiny was to fall in love with Jacques. An uncomplicated story of a friendship but, above all, the story of the uncompromising love of two men for the ocean.

Rosanna Arquette and Jean-Marc Barr during the shooting.

Jacques (Jean-Marc Barr) during one of his dives.

After weeks of reconnaissance by boat to discover the best island, the prettiest creek, and the most beautiful locations, shooting started in April 1987 in Lavendou. The crew then left for Taormina, followed by the Virgin Islands. On September 11th, they arrived in Amorgos, to the north of Santorini. The opening shots of the movie were filmed here. Jacques Mayol often came to visit the

crew as "technical advisor". Luc Besson telephoned him one day at his home in Marseilles, and they arranged to meet in Cassis, in a restaurant by the beach. An everyday type of conversation held around a table corner turned Jacques Mayol into a living legend. Magnificent footage, shot with humor tinged with sensitivity (Jean Bouise, Jacques' incredible uncle who dived into his bath and

Preceding double pages: *The two leading actors with Jacques Mayol, the real hero of the movie.*
Above: *Chozoviotissa monastery.*

Enzo, who slept in his diving suit), a close look at life, its aims and dreams, with that ama-zing and unforgettable scene where Jacques spends the night with the dolphins. The movie unleashed criticism at the Cannes Film Festival, but was nominated eight times for a Caesar award, received two, and became a legendary cult film for at least a whole generation.

Amorgos is undoubtedly the wildest island in the Cyclades. Its fantastic cliffs, plethora of pathways, the serenity of its villages, its olive groves and orchards all combine to give it that rare and strangely spiritual beauty. The superb Panaghia Chozoviotissa monastery that appears in the film, is located just behind Chora, the island's 'capital', pinned against a cliff 300 meters above the sea. It dates from the 11th Century and a few monks still live there, amongst their precious manuscripts and icons. Just below lies Haghia Anna beach, a superb turquoise blue creek in a majestic cliff setting. It will take you roughly ten minutes on foot to reach the little beach of Levroso and there you will find the "Aegialis Hotel". Built in 1991 near the striking village of Aegiali, it was the first major development on the Island. Irene Gianna-kopoulos and her husband Nikitas, both Greek, had the idea when Nikitas commented one day on the idyllic location and said, "we could build rather a nice little hotel here".

As always on the islands, this adventure turned out to be somewhat complicated. The hotel finally saw the day, nevertheless, in the purest Greek tradition. Between two sandy beaches, a group of immaculate dwellings with large bedrooms in shades of blue that Irene has deco-rated with pictures of Amorgos, with magnificent views

over the hills, the bay and the small island of Nikouria (where you can go out in a caique and sample delicious fish in the one and only small taverna), as well as a swimming pool with the sea at its foot. In the Sixties, Greek holiday-makers wanting to spend summer on the island were able to rent rooms overlooking the beach from Irene's father (at that time it was completely wild and unknown). Irene, her husband, and their son Stamatis have followed his example. You may even get married at the hotel, in accordance with Greek tradition or your own choice. Everything will be prepared for you amongst this splendid scenery.

After a day swimming in the creeks and perfecting your tan, there is nothing better than to settle down on the terrace with a traditional iced coffee. In the evening, when it gets milder, continue your excursion by strolling along the narrow shepherds' pathways to Tholaria, a delightful village with cobbled alleyways, or as far as Arkessini to the south, another typically Greek pheno-menon surrounded by olive trees and orchards, where the ruins of a superb ancient site still remain.

Millionaires are sometimes quite awe-inspiring adventurers. Not only did Howard Hughes launch Jane Russell, but he became one of the most brilliant pilots in the world and beat the world record during his crossing of the United States as well as by going around the world in 3 days and 19 minutes. The press magnate Malcolm Forbes traveled all over Malaysia, Thailand, Singapore, Brunei and then Japan in 1986 on his Harley Davidson. In 2001, the Californian millionaire Dennis Tito treated himself to the first 'tourist' excursion in space history and visited the universe aboard a Soyuz. One year later, the multi-millionaire Steve Fosset became the first man to go solo around the world in a balloon. He claims that he just asked himself one day what challenge there might be that he could possibly tackle. Richard Branson could have very well been Howard Hughes' co-pilot. At sixteen, he launched the magazine *Student*. At twenty, he founded Virgin Records to sell records by mail order. He then opened his first shop in London, creating cinemas, hotels, wedding dresses, a brand of soda, radio and airline company. In 1986, he pulverized the world record for crossing the Atlantic aboard his boat *Virgin Atlantic Challenger II*. The following year, he crossed the same ocean in his hot air balloon. In the midst of all that, he bought an island.

"During the Seventies, I was on a business trip when, during the course of a conversation, I heard about an island that was for sale. I also found out that it was possible to visit it. I found the idea quite amusing". Indeed, how could anyone resist such an opportunity? The place was located in the British Virgin Islands, to the east of Puerto Rico. Richard Branson longed to spend some time under the Caribbean sun. Moreover, everyone believed that the name of his company originated from these islands. He contacted the people in charge of the sale, who were not in the least bit surprised to see this young, barely twenty-two-year-old businessman turn up. Everything went extremely well to start off with at least. Upon his arrival in the Virgin Islands, the red carpet was rolled out for him. A limousine awaited him for his hotel transfer. A helicopter was available to take

NECKER ISLAND
(VIRGIN ISLANDS)

RICHARD BRANSON

• NECKER ISLAND •

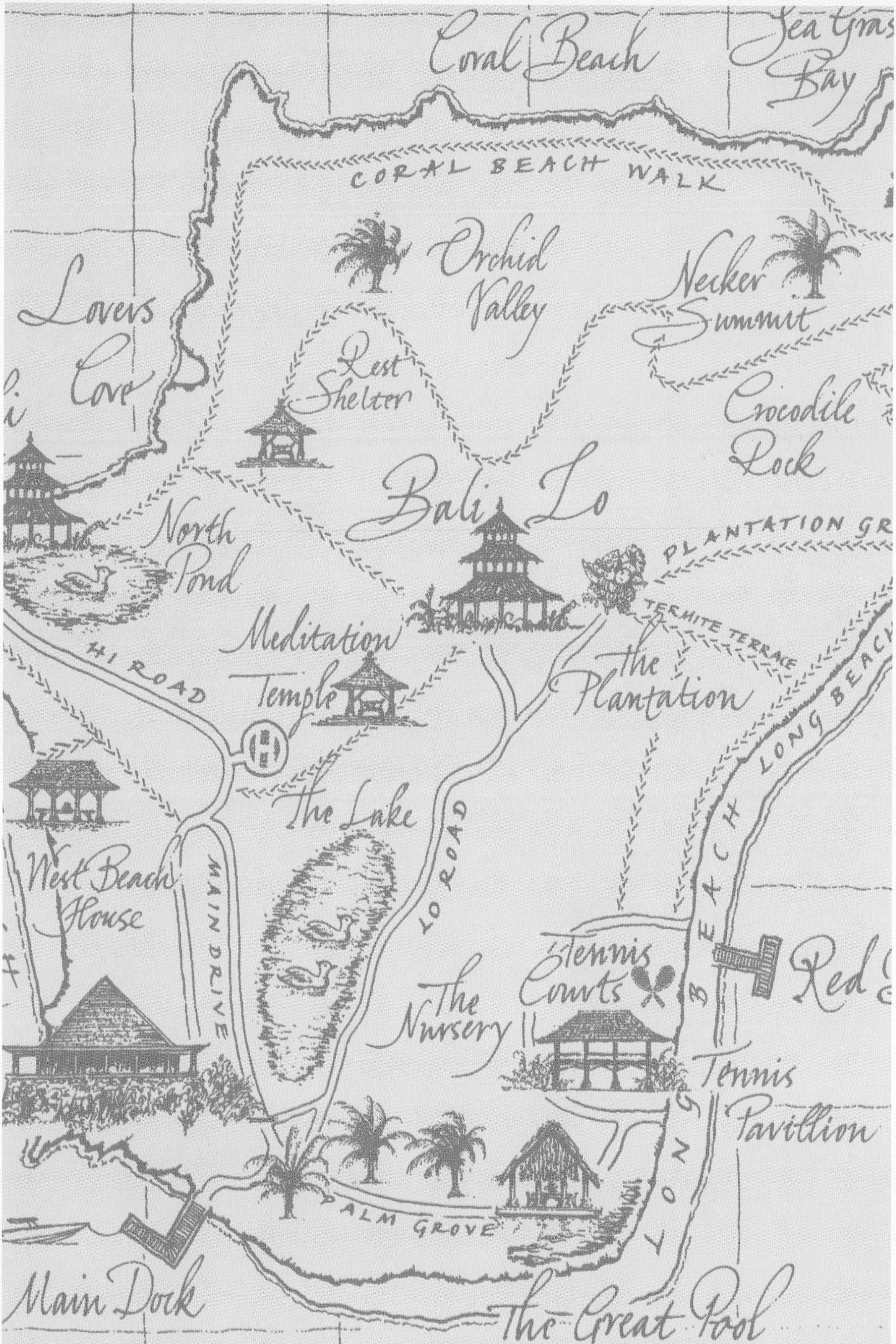

Coral Beach

Sea Grass Bay

CORAL BEACH WALK

Orchid Valley

Necker Summit

Lovers Cove

Rest Shelter

Crocodile Rock

North Pond

Bali Lo

PLANTATION GR

TERMITE TERRACE

Meditation Temple

the Plantation

HI ROAD

The Lake

LO ROAD

LONG BEACH

West Beach House

MAIN DRIVE

The Nursery

Tennis Courts

Red

Tennis Pavillion

L O N G   B E A C H

Palm Grove

Main Dock

The Great Pool

Map and bird's-eye view of Necker Island.

him for a tour of the region. The adventure thrilled him. Nevertheless, upon discovering the islands for the first time he was not very impressed. He later said that "they looked as if they were just pieces of rock emerging from the sea". Finally, they reached the one he was interested in. The sight of it appealed to him immediately. He informed the pilot that this was the island he wanted to buy: Necker Island. The pilot then told him what the price was. Richard Branson referred to an amount that he felt was more in line with his income at that time. The red carpet suddenly disappeared. He was taken back to the airport and even had to buy his own return ticket. While Steve Fossett attempted his trip around the world six times before he actually succeeded, Richard Branson did not have as long to wait. Two years later, the island was once again on the market. Only this time he had more than enough to purchase it.

The island had not been previously inhabited. To enhance

Bali atmosphere.

the sense of adventure, it had been used for a survival test during the Sixties. The famous war photographer Don Mc Cullin and one of his friends, Andrew Alexander, were left there without any food or water. They managed to survive only three weeks. When Richard Branson took possession of the place, everything was in need of attention. The island is magnificent, almost entirely surrounded by a divine coral reef barrier, mountains with cactus-topped peaks, and a stretch of exquisite, unspoiled beaches. It was completely wild and he wanted to turn it into a holiday home to spend some time with his family, get away from it all and live in perfect freedom. The island challenge was launched. Like others before him, he had everything brought over by boat, chose the best place to build, designed the interior decoration and developed the land. At last, he was able to spend the holiday he had so

longed for. The island provides a magical setting for the Balinese-style house: A superb salon, exotic dining room, ten bedrooms including a suite with private terrace, large white settees and colored silk cushions. Parts of the roof cleverly open out onto the boundless expanse of blue sky. The kitchen is enough to make even the most famous chefs go green with envy. The salon has the most up to date audio system, of course. The fantastic fresh water swimming pool is designed for guests to gather there for meals. Three other delightful houses were built soon after, also in the traditional Balinese style. Neverthe-less, Richard Branson quickly concluded that he was unable to go as often as he had hoped. It is sometimes difficult to combine myths and legends with reality.

Today this island is no longer a secret and has welcomed many famous guests attracted by the remoteness and the

magical setting so carefully created. Of the various islands that make up the British Virgin Islands, known as the "BVI", less than twenty are in fact inhabited: They contain everything necessary to attract visitors. Splendid coral reefs, tropical vegetation, white sandy beaches, deep creeks, volcanoes, and a thousand pirate stories in a setting that is a natural paradise as well as a tax haven. They belong to the British Crown but payments are in dollars. The atmosphere is both laid-back and cosmopolitan. The diving sites are famous all over the world. In addition, right next to Necker Island, there is another island for adventure, Norman Island, Robert Louis Stevenson's fabulous *Treasure Island* where, so the story goes, a treasure still lies hidden.

NECKER ISLAND
PO BOX 1091
THE VALLEY
VIRGIN GORDA
BRITISH VIRGIN ISLANDS
TEL.: + 1 (284) 494 2757
FAX: + 1 (284) 494 4396
necker@surfbvi.com
www.virgin.com/necker/

(prices per couple and per week) 9 rooms at $18,000, 1 suite at $19,400; Bali Lo residence: $20,300; Bali Hi and Bali Cliff residences at $22,600; Rental of the whole island: $22,500 per day (for between 1 and 14 guests), $28,500 per day (for between 15 and 20 guests), $36,000 per day (for between 21 and 26 guests). Restaurant, swimming pool, Jacuzzis, 2 tennis courts, gym, beauty salon, equipment for aquatic excursions …

How to get there
The easiest way is to land in Antigua, then take another flight for the island of Tortola and finally a ferry (30 minutes) to Necker Island.

ARCHIPELAGO OF ZANZIBAR

(TANZANIA)

EVELYN WAUGH

• FUNDU LAGOON •

Arriving at Fundu Lagoon.

Zanzibar is one of those places people dream of well before they ever visit them, sometimes without even knowing them. Jules Vernes took his characters in *Five Weeks in a Balloon* there without ever having been there himself. Joseph Kessel only stopped off there in his novel *The Lion*; Arthur Rimbaud talked about the place in his letters without ever going there either. In the same way like Macao or Valparaiso, just the name is enough to trigger off flights of fantasy. ZANZIBAR: The very word itself is captivating.

The island, or rather the two main islands that form the archipelago of Zanzibar, Unguja and Pemba, have always been priceless to navigators. Persians, Assyrians, Egyptians, Phoenicians, Portuguese, everything began with the slave, ivory and gold trade. In the 19th Century, cloves attracted other adventurers. The islands became the capital of the Oman Empire, under the control of the Sultan of Zanzibar. Mosques replaced Portuguese churches. The British took over from the Sultan in 1890. The slave treaty, the leopard skin trade, the spice trading ships with cloves, ginger, and cinnamon: Zanzibar became the "Island of Spices" and the dream became a myth. Explorers left their mark, including David Livingstone, the Scottish missionary, Richard Burton and John Speke seeking the source of the Nile. In October 1930, another

Englishman walked along these beaches, equally under its spell, the very English writer Evelyn Waugh, already a provocative, conservative ultra-snob. He wanted to attend the Emperor Hailé Sélassié's coronation, he set off for Abyssinia as correspondent for the *Times*. His journey took him much further after a voyage lasting four months. This gentleman liked to travel on an expense account. His articles published in *Harper's Bazaar* or the *Times* usually dealt with fashion, receptions, or the season in high society, but he also adored traveling on commission (he was always broke) and sent letters to his friends the Mitfords, the Churchills and Graham Greene from all over the world. On top of this, he did not want to have

Typical "boutre".

Evelyn Waugh in the Thirties.

anything to do with the telephone. Or rather, he treated it with contempt. "Write to me", he said to whoever wanted to contact him. Moreover, he knew how to discourage those of a rebellious nature. His letters, legible when he was sober and a little more obscure when he was tipsy, were like his books: corrosive, zany, alert, and an incredible eyewitness account of his time. At the end of the Twenties, his novel *Decline and Fall* made him famous. When he went to Zanzibar, he already had

his own distinctive way of expressing himself, tersely succinct. He arrived in Zanzibar in December "during the bad season". It was too hot. He booked in at the "English Club", nowadays "Africa House", where he spent his time sprinkling himself with quinine water before sitting under a ventilator. At night, he stayed awake and scarcely dared to turn his pillow over "to the dry side". He observed that everything was five minutes away on foot, commented on admirable staircases in houses, visited the

The very natural atmosphere at Fundu Lagoon.

Sultan's palace and remarked with his usual irony that British families lived in apartments with "things they had found in the Bazaar, cane armchairs and European children's toys". His escapade led him to the island of Pemba, to the northeast of Zanzibar "where there are only clove and coconut trees". A small boat, the *Halifa*, ensured the weekly crossing. He landed in the port of Mkoani, with a set of bungalows distributed here and there amidst verdant scenery. "Each pebble can be distinguished with incredible precision. I have never seen water as transparent". The sort of peregrinations that inspired him with *A Tourist in Africa* and *Remote People*. Once again a cocktail of the most exotic kind. The winding narrow streets in Stone Town, classified as World Cultural Heritage, with ancient buildings, superb balconies, amazing sculptured doors, mosques, ancient palaces,

Livingstone's house, the House of Wonders (the first building in Zanzibar to have electricity and a lift in the whole of East Africa), the divine Emerson & Green Hotel, and the Gardens of Salome, the last royal lineage. Each minute reveals more wonders for visitors to marvel at. Pemba, the island of cloves, is not far. The capital town bears the poetic name of Chake Chake. From there a track leads to little fishing villages and you can just imagine the Ngesi forest sheltering bush babies - those small, friendly, leaping lemurs, as well as all the other fauna and flora, the dhows, those typical boats described by Henri de Monfreid, the lively bazaar, turquoise lagoons, relics of a palace and cloves drying in the sun, and the dhow that takes you to Fundu Lagoon, inaccessible by road, with all that magic described so well by Evelyn Waugh.

Twenty bungalows have been built on the beach or above

in the hills, like tiny luxury cabins. The warm peaceful light will make you forget that there is another world. The simplicity of this idyllic setting is the work of its Scottish owner, Ellis Flyte, a designer and nomad with an inquisitive and subtle soul, forever dreaming of far-away seas and the ideal hideaway. She created this enchanting paradise with the help of the brothers, Alex and Marcus Lewis and the finance boffin Brian Henson. Large mosquito nets have been draped over beds covered in white linen, and the refined bathrooms, all in teak, reveal delectable beauty care products. The rustic wooden furniture is just perfect, made of bamboo, palm or other local trees, the large airy drapes, the lovely light range of clothes specially designed by Ellis, the African-patterned cushions, ornaments brought back from other trips, are all around you, the magnificent ocean, a diver's Eden, offer promises of precious souvenirs. The place is stylishly smart, and exclusively elegant. In a nutshell: cool. Evelyn Waugh could have written *A Bachelor Abroad* there.

FUNDU LAGOON
PEMBA
ZANZIBAR
TANZANIA
TEL.: + 255 (24) 223 2926
FAX: + 255 (24) 223 2937
fundu@africaonline.co.tz
www.fundulagoon.com

20 bungalows
at $240 during off-peak season
and $300 during peak season.
Restaurant and bars, diving club,
maritime excursions and safaris…

How to get there
From Zanzibar, a 3-hour flight
will bring you to Pemba
(3 flights every week)
or the ferry (daily).
The hotel ensures a daily
coach to Fundu Lagoon.

SRI LANKA
(INDIAN OCEAN)

"INDIANA JONES AND THE TEMPLE OF DOOM"

• THE DUTCH HOUSE DOORNBERG •

Entrance to the superb "Dutch House Doornberg".

Those who are under the impression that all islands look alike have never been to Sri Lanka, an island filled with mind-boggling jungle, forest, inextricable tree trunks, hills as green as the jungle dripping with a profusion of cascading verdure. Temples spring up from the shadows of the leaves that are invaded by butterflies and brightly colored birds. Villages line the earthen routes. Everywhere there are sounds and smells, beautiful sari-clad women and monkeys fighting over branches. A place for Indy, no doubt about that.

Everything started with a TV series that fascinated the young George Lucas. The adventures of a trooper archeologist that only stops at the words "to be continued". When he grew up the film director longed to make a movie out of this. He talked to his friend Steven Spielberg about it one day whilst they were lounging in the sun on a beach in Hawaii, and the project was launched.

They put the finishing touches to the character and his eventful journeys and added details inspired from the Bible, ancient legends and myths. In 1981, the first part of the saga propelled Dr. Jones, "expert in occult sciences and purveyor of rare antiques", to the rank of interplanetary hero, and made Harrison Ford, along with his fabulous sardonic smile, unforgettable. A "follow up" was necessary. In 1984, Henry "Indiana" Jones Junior, his

exact name, picks up his Stetson, his whip and leather jacket again, this time with his two associates by his side, the cabaret singer Willie (Kate Capshaw) and a malicious youngster. This was "Indiana Jones and the Temple of Doom". Five months of outdoor shooting, between California, Macao, Sri Lanka and the studios in England, with absolutely incredible settings, of course. The crew had hoped to shoot on the Wall of China but was unable to obtain the necessary authorization. They then thought about the Himalayas, but the place was covered with snow on the scheduled dates. Sri Lanka, with its incredible jungle scenery, turned out in the end to be the ideal place. During a helicopter reconnaissance over the island, the producer Robert Watts and the set designer Elliot Scott discovered a canyon near Kandy that was perfect for one of the scenes. The superb ancient town, the cultural and spiritual center of the island, its agreeable mountain cli-

Short Round and Dr. Jones.

mate, its majestic lake and its magnificent sacred temple, guardian of Buddha's tooth, enchanted them. In April 1983, the crew met up on the island to drink champagne for luck. This time the movie began in Shanghai in 1935. Indy had to flee after a very difficult negotiation. He found himself on the other side of the world with his companions, in a village from where a sacred stone had been stolen. The scene in Mayapor village was shot on the Hantane Tea Estate, a famous tea plantation and also a museum. The elephants came from the elephant orphanage in Pinnawela, another famous stopover near Kandy. Finally, the sequence where Indy finds himself in the middle of the liana bridge surrounded by his enemies, was shot above the canyon to the north

"Indy" in all his splendor.

Tea plantations in Sri Lanka.

of Kandy, on a specially built steel and cable bridge camouflaged by creepers and cords. After his adventure in Sri Lanka, Spielberg said, "I was astonished by the sounds there are in the jungle. I always thought that these noises were added by the MGM!"

The jungle is definitely not to be missed, and neither are the spice gardens, Nuwara Ellya, once upon a time a cool haven for the British, the fabulous precious stones, the old private clubs where you are still served by waiters in white gloves, the capital, Colombo, with its sophisticated boutiques such as Paradise Road, its tiny minute stalls and its mythical Galle Face Hotel, remains from the time when the island was called Ceylon. In addition, there is the divine Dutch House Doornberg, the new dream oasis for the adventurer. Upon arrival in Galle, the Old Dutch port to the south of the island, you have to climb up a tiny,

winding, isolated path. You hesitate for a moment. No hotel is in sight. Then the imposing gate appears and someone comes to open it with a superb smile. You follow a long graveled path, impeccably raked, and finish your journey in front of the magnificent renovated colonial house with a splendid Rover from the Forties parked in front, a perfect example of the style of Dr. Jones. After the heat, the dusty road, the mad traffic, the din, the freshness of the entrance delightfully stuns you. The place does justice to the magical history of the island, successively Sri Lankais, Portuguese, and English. A boutique-hotel, maybe, but above all an atmosphere of a tenderly loved private dwelling, where each and every detail is cared for to the extreme, where every object seems to have been carefully chosen to please each visitor, flowers and leaves, beautiful books and materials. The four suites, decorated

134

with rare talent, all open onto the garden and its luscious green lawn that, when needed, turns into a croquet pitch. Delightfully, graceful young girls watch over the travelers with charming gaiety, all Sri Lankan, bringing slices of fresh coconut and tea with carrot cake to guests relaxing around the swimming pool. Nothing is more exquisite than to stay there, with the feeling of being out of reach of the world's woes, worries and torments, surrounded only by the fantastic jungle full of placid, carefree monkeys. In the evening guests may relax with a Mango Martini in the salon before dining in the Sun House, the sister property lying just on the other side of the road. It feels as if a friend has acquired the house next door. Charming. Then, when the tropical heat has subsided, visitors will retire for the night and go to their rooms in a haze of amazement, and admire in wonder once more the view of the town stretching out in front of the house, before finally going to sleep underneath the cool blades of the fan.

THE DUTCH HOUSE DOORNBERG
C/o THE SUN HOUSE
23 UPPER DICKSON ROAD
GALLE
SRI LANKA
TEL.: + 94 (74) 380 275
FAX: + 94 (9) 22 624
sunhouse@sri.lanka.net
www.thesunhouse.com/doornberg.html

4 suites at $330.
Restaurant run by a Sri Lankan chef,
swimming pool, excursions to tea plantations,
elephant reserves and ancient cities...

How to get there
From Colombo airport, travel as far as Galle
by car or train (allow 3 hours for the trip).

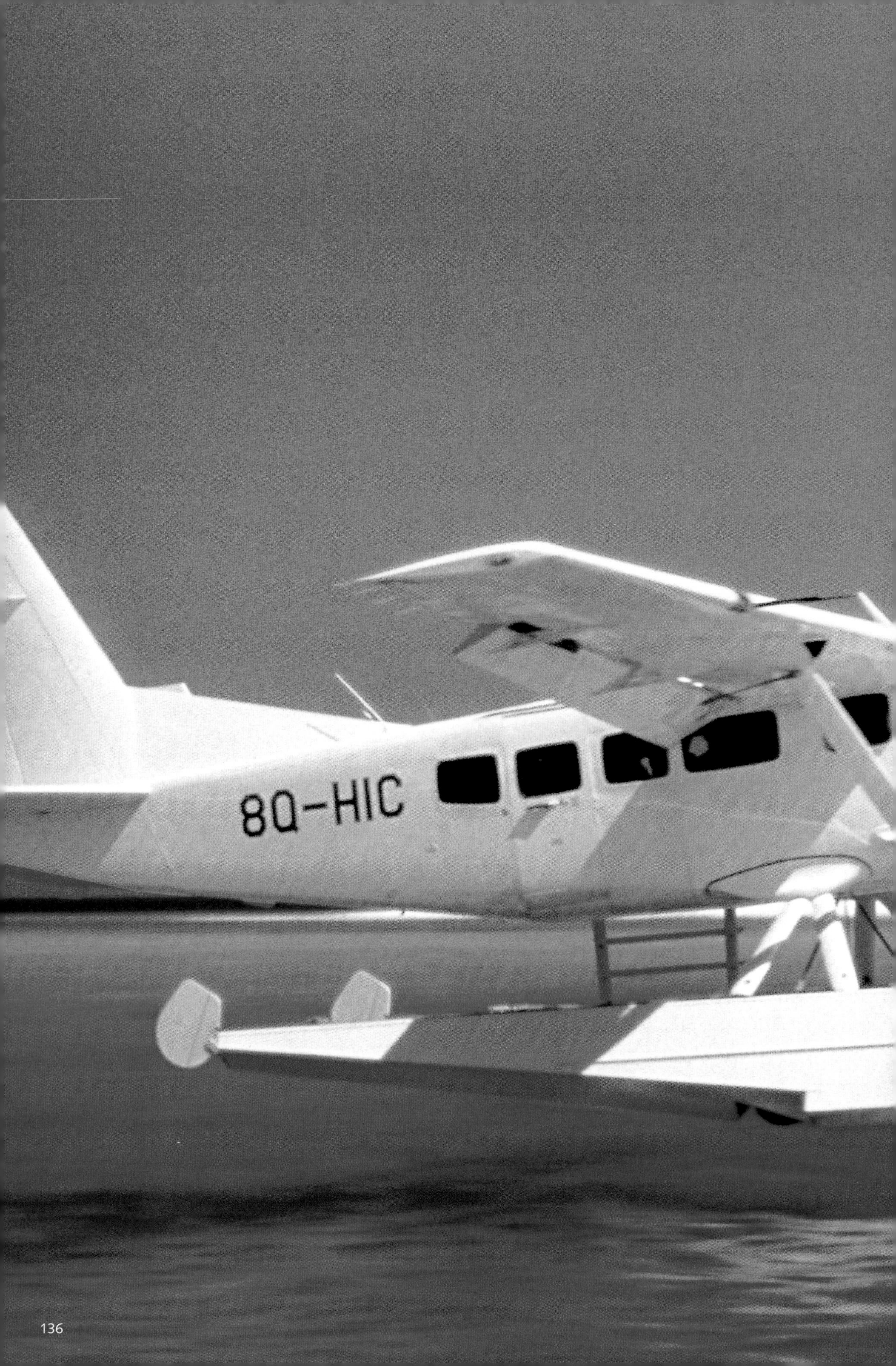
8Q-HIC

KUNFUNADHOO

(MALDIVES)

SONU & EVA SHIVDASANI

• SONEVA FUSHI ISLAND RESORT •

Above: *Eva Shivdasani in 2002.*
Opposite: *The shiny black bicycles in front of each bungalow at the Soneva Fushi Island Resort.*

Arrival at Kunfunadhoo is something that is truly unforgettable: The airline flight, followed by a trip in a hydra plane, glistening in the sun. Heat, at last. Barefoot pilots wearing white Bermuda shorts are full of smiles. Through a tiny window you catch your first glimpse of these remote islands, outlined in green, white, pink, turquoise and pale yellow. While skimming the water to land on a pier in the middle of the sea, a sign causing visitors to smile announces: Soneva Fushi International Airport. A white dhoni, the traditional boat, awaits you. Then a deliciously fresh coconut arrives, followed by a pretty canvas bag marked, "No News. No shoes". And there you are, the island you have so longed for appears before you and everything that reminds you of concrete is left at the bottom of your bag.

Sonu Shivdasani still remembers the reaction of his friends when he first talked about buying an island in the Maldives. "Nobody even knew where the Maldives were. They thought it was in Argentina!" However, Sonu appreciated challenges in the same way his famous father Indoo did, who built a conglomerate in Nigeria after studying in England. Sonu followed in his footsteps in his own way, using his Anglo-Indian education and the respect for others he inherited from his family to develop one of the most beautiful success stories in the field of tourism in the last few years, with the help of his Swedish wife Eva, whom he met in Monaco when she was a fashion model and a regular in the pages in *Vogue*.

One day they paid a visit to this lost corner of the world. This was right at the beginning of tourism to these fishing islands. "We slept in a very elementary place, with no air conditioning, not very comfortable. The food was bad. But it was fun", he said. Of course, the international airport was nothing like it is today, and none of the facilities that visitors today take for granted were available. The first hotel opened in 1974 in the Male atoll, sending food orders by radio to a central station that then got in touch with the supplier. Communication was by walkie talkie or using very approximate Morse code signals.

Eva and Sonu on their island-hotel.

Aerial view of Kunfunadhoo.

Means of transport were rudimentary. Aircrafts arrived on the little Hulhule runway on the neighboring island of Male that welcomed its first tourists in 1972. Twenty-two Italians fascinated by the location that had been previously seen only in a photograph. Nearly ten years later and over 33,000 tourists have landed on the tiny runway renamed the "International Airport of Male".

"From very early on we wanted to lease an island and build our own house", said Sonu, "but the government did not want us to occupy land that possibly had tourist potential, so we looked for an island on which we could build a small twenty-room hotel". However, nothing is ever as easy as that on islands, which constitutes part of their magnetic charm. "There were many islands we liked

but every time we revealed our concept, the site went to others who were planning a much larger development". Then they were offered Kunfunadhoo. "No one wanted it because it was too far from Male". A hotel had already been built on the island but had to close down after a few years because of transportation problems. At that time, in the Seventies, most local boats only had sails and it took around twenty-four hours to travel from Male to Kunfunadhoo. Sonu and Eva managed to create the island they had always dreamed of, gave it their name, established their own philosophy of life and turned it into a hotel. The Soneva Fushi, from Sonu and Eva with Fushi, which means "sand spit", opened in 1995. "Many people thought that the venture would not last more than two

The wildest Presidential suite in the world.

months, but we were confident. Even my mother was not very enthusiastic", recalls Sonu. "Until she came to the island". Today, all the glossy travel magazines of the world unceasingly shower praises on this island-hotel that bewitches even the most blasé. Particularly those who are seeking seclusion, as far away as possible from over-crowded schedules. I know of no other paradise that is more enchanting, where refinement is combined with so much poetry and imagination, that makes me feel so perfectly free, joyful and lighthearted. Firstly, there is the incredibly dense jungle, ecologically preserved in accor-dance with its owners' wishes to seduce your senses as they pour a hundred and one plant and flower fragrances over you as you ride on your bike in the morning, on your way to breakfast. Then all those precious details: the beautiful black bicycles in front of the bungalows, the

little engraved wooden signposts, the cottages on the sand, covered with exotic plants and flowers, the bar in bamboo also planted in the sand, the computer room is in a wooden cabin perched high in the trees. Time has even been especially changed to be in line with the sun so that visitors can enjoy more of it! No shoes. No showing off. No outward signs of anything. No trying to make an appearance or be noticed. Simplicity, anonymity and free-dom are the determining factors for the clientele. The day starts with the "click-clack" of the geckos, tiny inoffensive lizards that are the island's mascots. No oppressive beasts, just a few crows and some very polite white rabbits. Go swimming, or read. Wander lazily under the shade of the palm trees. Take a nap or just relax doing nothing, absolutely nothing. Just for pleasure, abandon yourself to the fabulous "Six Senses" spa team who, in a setting

of stone and waterfalls, will chase away any remaining stress, facing the translucent ocean and those most beautiful ultra famous depths. A thousand species of fish, skates of all sorts, uninhibited sea turtles that swim around just two yards from the shore, incredible corals. Diving in the Maldives no longer needs any publicity. All divers dream of the Maldives and Thomas, the Swiss Soleni Dive Center manager, is always welcoming passionate lovers of diving who return, enchanted by the incredible sights, and that special kind friendliness shown by the Japanese girl, Saki, the Spaniard Sebastian and all his extremely professional team. It is difficult to believe that a so-called expert once said that the Maldives offered no tourist potential!

Sonu and Eva have created their island, with sensitivity, discernment, humor and sincerity but without taking themselves too seriously. To say that they have dreamt up the perfect island is the understatement of the year.

BALI
(INDONESIA)
NOEL COWARD
• BEGAWAN GIRI ESTATE •

The wonderful Bali wildlife.

The world of the Thirties: The era of the Spanish War, the New Deal, Technicolor, television, nylon and cellophane. Distances were shrinking fast. The Queen Mary crossed the Atlantic Ocean in a record time of three days and twenty-one hours. The Orient Express rapidly linked Paris to Istanbul. Heroes were Mahatma Gandhi, Jean Harlow, Jesse Owens and Noel Coward, or rather Sir Noel Coward. They say he invented the Englishman: elegant, funny and fashionable. British right down to his fingertips and a dandy from head to toe, he who came from a modest a London suburban family. Actor, playwright, virtuoso pianist, composer, writer, humorist and much more, he reigned over the Thirties and fascinated the beautiful people, coining the expression "Café Society" for those now referred to as the Jet Set. From the scenario of *Brief Encounters* to *Private Lives*, including his *Poor Little Rich Girl* and unforgettable musical comedies, he told a thousand tales, wrote a hundred songs, boosted the morale of his contemporaries many a time, and in turn became the most famous, most sophisticated, most entertaining and, above all, the most charming Englishman of his time. His life: sophisticated, productive, exhausting. Work, cocktails, lovers, travel. He took every opportunity to travel, preferably as far away as possible, to take a step back and think, to forget about society, and to slow down

as he knew that his pace had become chaotic. These were his only real moments of privacy and intimacy, a habit that he kept up until quite late in his life. In 1927, he went to Hawaii, and then Tokyo, Peking, Angkor, Shanghai, Hong Kong, Korea, Manchuria and Vietnam. Another time his travels took him to Bali, one of those classic stopovers of the time with Ceylon, Singapore (and the Raffles Hotel, of course) and Java. Everybody who was somebody went to Indonesia, especially to Ubud, the village that bred artists and intellectuals, situated in the center of the island: actors, aristocrats and personalities who had both time and money. The Canadian composer Colin McPhee even set up home there, bringing over his piano and writing *A House in Bali* whilst absorbing the magnificent scenery. The German artist

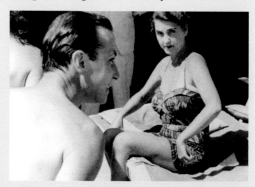

The heiress Barbara Hutton, who also fell under Bali's spell.

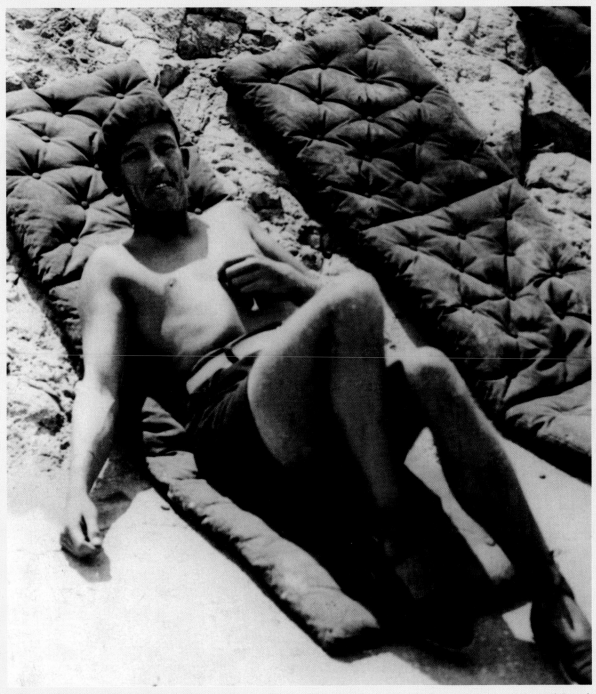

Sir Noel Coward.

Walter Spies also ended up living on the island and his house can still be visited today, as did Charlie Chaplin and Paulette Godard, the heiress Barbara Hutton, the novelist Vicky Baum, Gloria Vanderbilt, the Mexican artist Miguel Covarrubias, as well as Margaret Mead and Gregory Bateson, the intrepid pioneers of anthropology who went to study a Bali family for two years.

The bohemian style and the artistic atmosphere enthralled them all. "Each Balinese is creative", wrote Noel Coward to his friend Charlie Chaplin, "from the womb to the tomb, from sunrise till after sundown. They sculpt, they paint, and they practice their songs." Many people believe that Bali reached the height of its artistic fame at that time. There were famous sacred dancing shows to attend, temples to be visited. Travelers stayed at the luxurious Bali Hotel in the capital Denpasar, at about forty-five minutes from Ubud, crossing the island by car. Things have changed but Ubud has remained an artistic hideaway surrounded by the rice fields that so captivated travelers in the Thirties.

Preceding double pages: *"The Source", Begawan Giri Estate's spa.*
Above: *Eight hectares of elegance.*

Stories abound of rice paddies, of markets overflowing with kebab vendors, of the Monkey Forest, a tiny jungle populated by bold monkeys, art galleries, artists' studio workshops, museums such as the Puri Lukisan and its amazing garden. The artists are still there. You can still see the dance shows that charmed Noel Coward and his friends so much and that still cause a sensation both for visitors and inhabitants.

Then there are the countless beautiful guesthouses, often the work of artists, and fabulous hotels such as the Begawan Giri Estate, the Wise Man's Mountain, right near Ubud, looking as if it had just emerged from the jungle one morning, naturally and silently. The word hotel is not quite the right expression either. Begawan Giri Estate is a private domain comprising eight hectares of luxurious gardens, with five quite remarkable residences called

Bayugita ("Song of the Wind"), Tirta-Ening ("Clear Water") and Wanakasa ("Forest in the Mist")... names inspired by the location, decoration, atmosphere and style. Guests can reserve a whole residence or just book a suite. A majordomo has been chosen for each residence "who looks after guests as if they were my best friends in my own house". Luxury straight out of a novel in a setting of hand crafted doors, stone sculptures, English 19th Century pieces depending on the room, outside showers, private swimming pools, bamboo beds, old teak wainscoting, views over rice fields and fabulous scenery "welcoming yet not too impressive", as Somerset Maugham wrote.

Every minute detail, right down to the spa that suggests harmonious and poetic promenades down the River Ayung, is a reminder of a tradition, an intrinsic part of Bali's history. This island located between Asia and

Australia, looks a little lost amongst the 13,000 islands in this archipelago, the biggest in the world. The Chinese navigator Cheng Ho was the first to open the route in 1405, at the head of a gigantic fleet carrying nearly 28,000 men including sailors, administrators, interpreters, doctors and soldiers, as well as silk, porcelain, pieces of silver, and cotton. He made seven different journeys, visited thirty-seven countries, sometimes taking up to 30,000 men on board. Famous in China, he traveled all over this part of the world well before the Dutch and any of the sophisticated visitors, often using tools as simple as incense sticks graduated to measure time.

BEGAWAN GIRI ESTATE
PO BOX 54
UBUD 80570
BALI
INDONESIA
DESIGN HOTELS
TEL.: + 62 (361) 978 888
FAX: + 62 (361) 978 889
reservations@begawan.com
www.begawan.com

22 suites from $475 to $2,950,
Entire residences from $2,375 to $4,400
(with private swimming pool and Jacuzzi).
Biji restaurant, The Source spa, excursions,
medical assistance …

How to get there
From Denpasar international airport (on Bali),
Ubud lies only 45 minutes away by car.

FIJI

(OCEANIA)

"THE BLUE LAGOON"

• TURTLE ISLAND •

A lost island in the Fiji archipelago, a shipwreck that left two children imprisoned in an unknown world. The school of life. In 1908, the Irish writer and doctor, Henri de Vere Stacpoole published *The Blue Lagoon*. He was a country doctor, and author of several novels, living in Somerset. In 1907, he woke up one night, distressed and unable to sleep. He suddenly envied primitive men who in their ignorance were dazzled simply by the rising sun or the appearance of the moon. He thought to himself that civilization had unveiled all the great mysteries of the universe whilst giving birth to indifference, and he felt a great surge of awe of something. His job had accustomed him to all of life's events. He lamented the fact that he no longer felt any emotion and was not moved by life, death or birth. One thought gave rise to another, and in the morning, he found himself writing *The Blue Lagoon – A Romance*, the story of two innocent children confronted with life's momentous occasions. In 1907, Stacpoole showed his manuscript to the publisher T. Fisher Unwin. Published in 1908, the book was acclaimed by critics. It was a fresh story, with the extremely vivid descriptions of the islands and their inhabitants that Stacpoole knew well from his experience as ship's doctor. The press raved and the public were equally enthusiastic.

In 1923, Hollywood shot the motion picture, a silent black and white movie. In 1949, the story was filmed again by the English film director, Frank Launder, this time in technicolor starring the actress Jean Simmons. In 1980, Brooke Shields played the part of Emmeline, one of the two children abandoned on the island. This movie was shot in Jamaica and Turtle Island, "Nanuya Levu" in the South Pacific. A tiny speck on the map to the east of Australia, in the Yasawa archipelago, it was famous all over the word for its splendid scenery. Stacpoole's story was abridged in order to highlight the sensuality of the adventure and the spectacular setting. Brooke Shields had just finished shooting *Pretty Baby* with Louis Malle. Everybody remembered her unforgettably appealing face and suggestive poses. All that was required was an idyllic setting to maintain the fantasy: Wonderful white beaches, truly turquoise sea, flamboyantly colored parrots, a universe of plants and flowers and a barely clad actress. Truly a motion picture postcard. A sexy journey, easily

Christopher Atkins and Brooke Shields during the shooting.

Brooke Shields in "The Blue Lagoon" by Randal Kleiser (1980).

made to fantasy's outer limits. Nestor Almendros, photography director, who had worked on most of Francois Truffaut's films as well as on *Sophie's Choice*, *Kramer vs. Kramer*, *The Days of Heaven* and other famous motion pictures, had been awarded Oscars for his sets. The picture of the ideal couple in dream scenery was featured on the cover of *People* Magazine. Even today, you need only to say the words "Blue Lagoon" to conjure up a vision of an island with mythical countryside.

Every day, reality is there bathed in sun, luxurious, and deep down in the depths of the tropics. Turtle Island is the work of Richard Evanson, an American from Washington. After making a fortune in cable TV, he bought the island in 1972, having decided to escape to a place as far away as possible from civilization. He still reaps the rewards for his work in favor of the environment. A foundation, The Island Community, has put the finishing touches to his efforts, enabling him to open clinics, schools, to improve

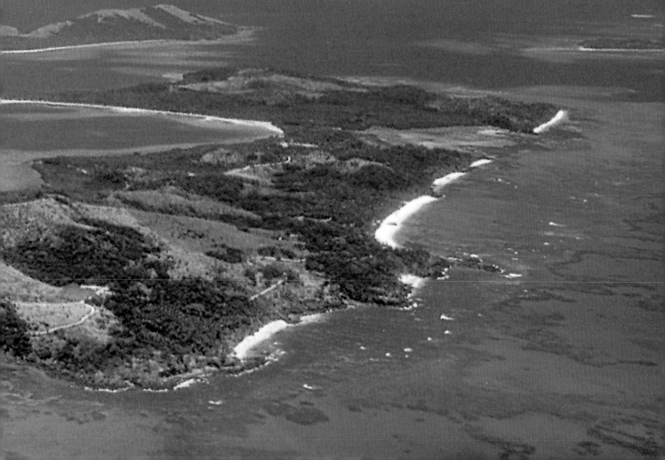

Opposite: *Scene from "The Blue Lagoon" by Frank Launder with Jean Simmons (1949).*

the quality of the water and public transport in the villages and surrounding islands. When Columbia Pictures was looking for the ideal island on which to shoot *The Blue Lagoon*, Turtle Island very quickly appeared at the top of the list.

Richard Evanson kept some of the houses built for the movie. Only fifteen couples may stay at any one time in the characteristic "bures" built on the water's edge, superb faithful replicas of traditional Fijian dwellings. With an impressive floor to ceiling height, each of them has a living room, separate bedroom, dressing room and bathroom, all decorated with handcrafted objects built from local materials, luxury combined with nature for a harmonious setting. In one, there is a large four-poster bed with white linen sheets and magnificent light wood pillars. In another, small bedside tables resemble tree

trunks. The larger bures have a Jacuzzi, outside showers, and a verandah underneath the palm trees with an enormous bed for siesta time. All are sufficiently separated to provide that dream of intimacy. A single track wanders through the trees around the island without disturbing the vegetation. The blue lagoon exists of course, carved out by nature, and the realm of corals, fish or "frangipane groves", dense forests, volcanic cliffs, wild mountains, green lagoons and magical views. The 250- hectare island offers plenty of options: Diving, horse riding, boat trips, kayaking, windsurfing, quiet evenings by the sea and mountain excursions where unique panoramic views await discovery. Or visit the fourteen white beaches, some of which are completely isolated. You may feel as if you are living a thousand miles away from the rest of the world.

In 1643, the Dutchman Abel Tasman was the first to dare

venture into these high seas. Only James Cook and William Bligh, Captain of *The Bounty* followed him some hundred years later. Time has not conquered this magnificent remoteness.

Guests may dive on the floating pier, where an intimate meal can be enjoyed with no one else around, bathed only by the soft light of the moon and the lanterns. Others may wish to reserve a whole beach just for themselves, and have a picnic hamper complete with wine, champagne and other delicacies brought to them. Privacy and peace, seclusion and sand, with wind blown palm trees. Turtle Island is a place for the romantic and the perfect setting for a honeymoon.

TURTLE ISLAND
LEVEL 1, 38-40 GARDEN STREET
SOUTH YARRA, VIC. 3141
AUSTRALIA
SMALL LUXURY HOTELS OF THE WORLD
TEL.: + 61 (3) 9823 8300
FAX: + 61 (3) 9823 8383
info@turtlefiji.com.au
www.turtlefiji.com

15 "bures" from $1,124 to $1,646
(off-peak season),
and from $1,236 to $1,810 (peak season).
Restaurant, botanic garden, boat trips,
diving, riding, kayak, possibility for a couple
to reserve a private beach …

How to get there
At the Nadi international airport, the Turtle Island
office will organize your
connecting flight.

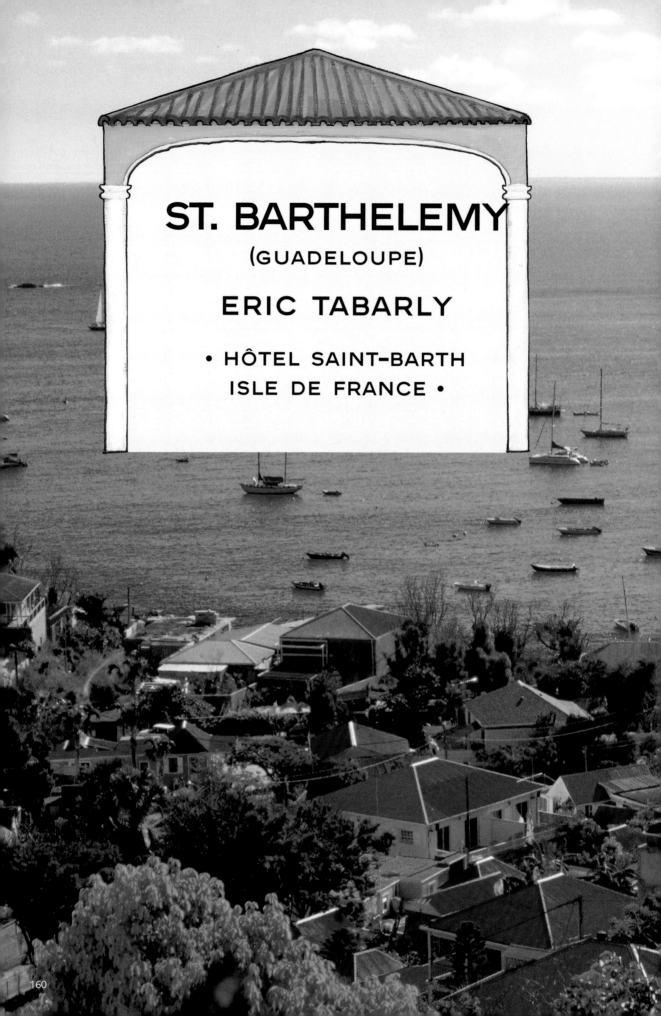

ST. BARTHELEMY

(GUADELOUPE)

ERIC TABARLY

• HÔTEL SAINT-BARTH
ISLE DE FRANCE •

The magnificent Anse du Colombier beach.

The ritual is famous and unchanging. Visitors climb aboard a little "old crate" in either Guadeloupe or St. Martin, a short flight above crystal clear waters, then the runway appears, a pocket handkerchief stuck between sea and mountain that causes passengers to question whether the aircraft will ever make it. Yet, the aircraft lands each time on an airfield the size of a breadcrumb, the only place on the island that is flat. Christopher Columbus discovered this pearl of the French West Indies in 1493 and named it after his brother Bartholomeo. The Norman and Breton colonists came afterwards, then the Swedish, briefly followed by the British. The French finally recuperated it in 1878 after a referendum with 351 votes against 1. All have left their trace. The Swedish transformed it into a free port, turning it into a prosperous land. The French gave it their language. All of them brought their light skin.

In Spring 1989, Eric Tabarly landed there. He was taking part in the double Transatlantic Race "Lorient-St. Barthelemy-Lorient" aboard a "new generation trimaran" with his friend Jean Le Cam. He departed from Brittany, France and arrived in Gustavia, the island's capital and harbor, passing through the ever-dreaded Bay of Biscay, then returning the other way around. The world-famous navigator later wrote in his "Ocean Journal" that the only time he had been truly scared as a sailor was on this boat, at the age of fifty-eight. He who had lined up victory after victory, who had been instrumental in showing the whole world what sailing was about, who had sailed across every ocean, found this "modern" boat difficult to handle. He missed his *Pen Duick*, the revolutionary yacht that he had designed himself. At the St. Barthelemy halt, Eric Tabarly met up with his Martinique wife and his daughter, relaxed, taking advantage of the island where his native Brittany and the tropics are both reunited. In addition, every time the race arrives, the island organizes a thousand festivities. Nautical parades, evenings of folklore, fireworks. Streets are crowded with people who meet up in hotels and restaurants to comment on the event. You can get several days of such partying only the islands. The sailor took pleasure in mixing with the crowd and his admirers.

May 31st, 1968: Eric Tabarly on board "Pen Duick IV", before the 1968 Solo Translatlantic Race (from Plymouth to Rhode Island).

In contrast to what many people think, he was both talkative and friendly. It all depended on the person he was talking to, said one of his friends. Nevertheless, during the return journey, the adventure took another direction. "Everything happened very quickly", he wrote. "You cross the point of no return in no time at all, without having any time to react". His crewmate was on the radio whilst he was trying to hold the helm. It was impossible. The boat keeled over and the two friends had to wait six hours before anyone came to collect them. "It was the only time I was frightened", he said afterwards. "I didn't have time on the other occasions ".

St. Barthelemy, or St. Barts or Barths as it is more affectionately known, still fascinates navigators as well as

Swimming pool at the Hôtel Saint-Barth Isle de France.

celebrities and its anchorage is famous globally. As soon as your feet touch the ground at St. Jean airport the place will enchant you, with its adorable pastel colored cottages and the infectiously good-humored manner with which you are welcomed. As well as greeting new arrivals, people come to collect packages or to hear the news. All the good humor of the French West Indies is there.

David Rockefeller, Rudolf Nureyev, Baryshnikov, fashion photographers, cinema gentry have all fallen under the spell of these charming pale pink, bright yellow and sky blue houses of the very stylish cosmopolitan High Street where Avenue Montaigne or Madison Avenue brands are neighbors, of the beaches, the tropical gardens, the frightfully chic restaurants, and the delightfully colored mini mokes that travel all over the Island. All seek its peace and tranquility, its relaxed bohemian elegance, its Caribbean

Island atmosphere mingled with that St. Tropez glamour. Those discreetly elegant hotels quietly competing with each other. Hôtel Saint-Barth Isle de France is one of the jewels in Anse des Flamands that has the reputation of owning one of the island's most beautiful beaches. The superb plantation-style mansion facing the sea is hidden amongst a forest of "latanier" trees, St. Barts' palm tree emblem. The large cool white bedrooms look over the ocean or the palm grove. Amongst a tangle of vegetation and flowers, charming plantation style bungalows await discovery, built right next to the white beach. Less than a minute from the sea, there is also a small angler's house with its own garden. The small blue wooden shop is quite adorable. The menu of the restaurant "La Case de l'Isle" is utterly delicious. The antique furniture and the remarkable simplicity of each enchanting detail, a beautiful vase

on each table, with bright orange "balisiers", is characteristic of the French West Indies, as is the small flaming fiery red branch on your pillow. Outdoors, a soft mixture of blue and white surrounding the swimming pool gives the impression of extending as far as the sea. Spend the day at the Anse des Cayes, both a surfers' and divers' paradise, or the Anse du Colombier, with its magnificent hidden beach, where the opportunity to go swimming amongst coralline fish is not to be missed. Meet up in Gustavia for a drink at the terrace of Le Select, the island's bar since time immemorial, forever welcoming both celebrities and navigators. You can buy T-shirts with "Sorry-No telephone" on them, whilst admiring yachts lying in anchorage there. Without a doubt, both leading sailors and the world's most sophisticated yachts have not finished casting anchor in St. Barts.

HÔTEL SAINT-BARTH ISLE DE FRANCE
BAIE DES FLAMANDS
PO BOX 612
97098 ST. BARTHELEMY CEDEX
GUADELOUPE
TEL.: + 59 (05) 90 27 61 81
FAX: + 59 (05) 90 27 86 83
isledefr@saint-barths.com
www.isle-de-france.com

33 rooms, including 5 suites and 13 bungalows, from $471 to $612 (during off-peak season), from $682 to $910 (during peak season). La Case restaurant, tennis court, 2 swimming pools, excursions by boat or on horseback.... *Attention: closed between 1st September and 15th October every year.*

How to get there
From St. Martin or Pointe-à-Pitre, fly to St. Barth (no flights after sunset), or by sea.

PHUKET

(THAILAND)

"THE BEACH"

• THE CHEDI PHUKET •

The Chedi Phuket.

Phuket Island appeared on the map in 1970. The world suddenly woke up and realized that the earth was polluted. People began to panic after the radioactive leakages from the Three Mile Island nuclear power plant in Pennsylvania, and the tons of oil dispersed all over the Brittany coasts by the *Amoco Cadiz*. In London, Friends of the Earth marched in protest against paper wastage. In the USA, Vietnam War veterans threw away their medals. Jane Fonda left for Hanoi. Legislation on marijuana was requested. Refusal to continue to accept the world as it was came from all over the earth. Phuket Island seemed to be the reply, along with Kathmandu, Goa, and Marrakech. Friendly places, where ecology is not just a dream, where it is good to be able to live freely in the sun, far away from the "system". The hippies took over the island. In no time at all it became the hedonistic solution: a haven of spirituality, a place for rediscovering yourself, the clean world as it should never have ceased to exist. The legend had begun.

However, it did not stop there. In 1997, Alex Garland, a young Londoner and untiring globe trotter, published a novel inspired from his own experience, *The Beach*. The book was highly acclaimed and was translated into 25 languages, appearing at the top of the best seller lists everywhere in the world. It told the story of Richard, who,

just like hippies in the Seventies, was haunted by the idea of the initiation trip. After a journey to Asia, he arrived in Bangkok where he met a rather odd sort of person who told him about an ideal island, an undiscovered paradise. Accompanied by a couple of friends, Richard decided to set off for the longed-for Eden, that was very shortly going to turn into Hell.

The book was such a success that it was adapted for the screen in 1999 with Leonardo Di Caprio in the leading role. "We were looking for an island paradise. We discovered Phi Phi Leh, a tiny island just off Phuket. The cliffs protect its beach of fine sand and its lagoon is spectacularly beautiful. It was the ideal location". The film director Danny Boyle did not hesitate for one moment. Phuket, Phi Phi Leh and the surrounding region provided all the scenery he had

The French girl (Ledoyen) who accompanied Richard in his quest.

168

Leonardo DiCaprio in "The Beach" (1999).

dreamed of. The movie travels from Bangkok and the famous Khao San Road (a not to be missed break in any travelers' journey), to the Andaman Sea, to Phi Phi Leh Island and to southwest Phuket. The splendid Khao Yai National Park, a famous nature reserve situated approximately two hours away from Bangkok, was used to shoot the waterfall scene when the hero arrives on the island for the first time. It is one of the largest national parks in the country, an exceptional site regrouping 153 different species of animals, a jungle that is quite unspoiled, and wild

orchids that you can also admire in the superb Orchid Garden in Phuket.

The hero discovered the magnificent white beach of Maya Bay, harpoon fishing in the transparent lagoon just two paces from the shore. Strangely enough, the atmosphere prevalent during the shooting was like the atmosphere of the book and of the movie itself. Thirty-odd people on an island, cut off from the rest of the world. A hothouse atmosphere where you have to cohabitate with Mother Nature all around you. The Thai Navy patrol monitored

Preceding double pages and above: *Phi Phi Leh.*

the comings and goings of the crew as well as the equipment that was brought over by ferry to the island daily, to ensure that the scenery, countryside and corals were not damaged. The environmental experts did not take their eyes off the shooting either. There was the very real sensation of living in another world.

The Phi Phi Islands – Phi Phi Don and Phi Phi Leh – still retain the same charm, with their cliffs, little fishing villages, deep bays, and rustic bungalows. This is where the famous sparrows' nests are to be found – clinging to the sides of the spectacular grottoes – that Chinese restaurants all over the world are so fond of, and that the reckless collect by hanging onto the rocks. Phuket is still on the map. The hippies from the Seventies started the guest house fashion and the world followed by building hotels on the beaches where they slept. The Chedi

Phuket, in Pansea Bay, is one of the most beautiful success stories of the island, with its stunning thatched roof cottages spread around under the cool shade of the palm trees, its light rooms in teak, from where the sound of the waves can be heard, its simple and pure elegance. The spectacular swimming pool nearly reaches down as far as the sea. The sandy white beach lies at the foot of the dainty cottages. The luxuriant vegetation and the perfect view of sand and sea appear to have been tailor-made to soothe even the most over excitable of visitors, whilst waiting for a fabulous Honey Release Massage.

In Phuket, you can visit the islands from the hotel, which also organizes walks to other famous sites, such as Phang Nga Bay where *The Man with the Golden Gun* was filmed. And then there is the wonderful Thai cooking, yellow, red and green curries, flavored with garlic, sesame, tamarind,

ginger, coconut milk, mint and lemongrass, a celebration of talent displayed in all three of the hotel restaurants.

In Phuket, former trading place of the kingdom of Siam, much appreciated by traders in Asia as well as by buccaneers, visitors can wander from the Thai temples to the evening markets.

Nowadays, Chiang Mai, the former hippie town, welcomes travelers as well as those for whom Phuket remains a distinctively unique island. For such discerning guests, the "Eagle Guest House" organizes fabulous treks through the depths of the jungle or dense forest, an elephant ride, a trip on a bamboo raft to spend your last night staying in a house on stilts with a mountain tribe! Under these conditions, it is quite impossible not to feel as if you are miles away from everything!

THE CHEDI PHUKET
PANSEA BAY 118 MOO 3
CHOENGTALAY
TALANG, 83110 PHUKET
THAILAND
DESIGN HOTELS
FREE PHONE NUMBER : + 1 (800) 33 74 46 33
TEL.: + 66 (76) 32 40 17
FAX: + 66 (76) 32 42 52
augsburg@designhotels.com
www.designhotels.com

108 rooms from $160 to $780.
3 restaurants, large swimming pool,
spa, 2 tennis courts, aquatic sports…

How to get there
From Bangkok, various bus companies
offer several daily departures to Phuket.
Thai Airways also provides 10 daily return flights
to Phuket and back (1 hour 25-minute flight).
The hotel is situated 20 minutes
from the center of Phuket
and 25 minutes from Phuket airport.

IBIZA
(THE BALEARES)

"MORE"

• HOTEL HACIENDA –
NA XAMENA •

Hotel Hacienda - Na Xamena: a unique location, patiently designed by its owner, Alvar Lipszyc.

Ibiza keeps its secrets well hidden. Those lost creeks, crystalline water, little paths forgotten by tourists, that magnificent scenery, the magic of the Balearic Islands: Nothing is visible to the naked eye. Ibiza also knows how to look after its myth. The Seventies, flower power, long-haired hitchhikers, artificial heaven, the era of Katmandu, of love not war, of dreams as only luggage, all part of a hedonistic lifestyle. Beatniks and then Hippies turned the journey into a great Pacific adventure via Marbella, Mykonos, Goa, the States and Ibiza. They marched against war in Vietnam whilst listening to Jimi Hendrix, Jefferson Airplane, and Pink Floyd. Dennis Hopper woke up the planet with *Easy Rider* and his heroes with their crazy choppers. The big happening of the following year was created by Barbet Schroeder presenting *More* at the Festival of Cannes with its hallucinogenic trips.

This cult movie, the first made by the film director, was shot on the island, with blinding summer sunlight for the opening scenes. Stephen, a student from Lübeck attracted by the sun, falls in love with Estelle (the stunning Mimsy Farmer), who draws him into her world of overindulgence in Ibiza. A straightforward story of a psychedelic universe, broken rules and lives. Sex, drugs and rock 'n' roll. A vision of youth at the time, avid for extreme sensations and pleasures, when AIDS was unheard of and posed no threat. They settle in a large white house overlooking the turquoise blue sea to the south of the island, swim naked in the natural creeks, sunbathe on the rocks, wear transparent tunics and embroidered jackets just as people still do today, and little by little drifted away.

Schroeder said he wanted to bury some of his own past with this movie. He asked the already famous Pink Floyd to compose the sound track for the motion picture. The album took a week to compose and was banned in England, adding to the group's torrid reputation. Birds warbling, an atmosphere of peace, whispering, flute, organ, flamenco guitar and that inspired song "Ibiza Bar"... All the atmosphere of the island was encapsulated there, wrapped up in the glorious Mediterranean sun.

Sex, drugs and rock 'n' roll...

Mimsy Farmer as Estelle.

Thirty years later Ibiza still has this atmosphere of peace, inspiration and the mixture of styles. Phoenicians, Arabs, Moors, Berbers, Catalans, artists from every walk of life, American boys escaping the Vietnam war, New Age adepts, all contributed to dissimilarity, achieving a rarely found tolerance. Only one belief: Everyone can do whatever he wants in his own house. The architecture confirms this philosophy. Fincas have whitewashed walls. Few openings. Properties fenced in by low stone walls.

The inhabitants of Ibiza are individualists. This penchant for protection has preserved the island, because Ibiza is a mini paradise. To discover this you will need to depart from well-known paths. Along the San Miguel coast as far as the "so famous" Salines beach, chock full with people in summer, you will find only tiny crystal clear water creeks, wild paths and all-white villages with their rural churches. In September and October, when there are only shepherds and peasants in the countryside, the island can

177

Private swimming pool of one of the Hotel Hacienda - Na Xamena rooms.

be seen as it really is: superb, natural, surprising both by its peaceful tranquility and charm.

The Hotel Hacienda Na Xamena in San Miguel adds to this attraction. The road will fascinate you with its pine trees tightly lined up one against the other, and its sinuous track, to a unique location, patiently designed by its owner. Alvar Lipszyc came from Belgium with his architect father during the Fifties. He remembers his father's first words: "This sensation, we must share it with others". The hotel was built. In turn, Alvar became an architect and has since pursued the family dream. Each year has brought a new project, a new detail. Both he and his wife, Sabine, a beauty from northern France who is as enthusiastic as himself, wanted a hotel of human dimensions. Having observed during a stay in Bali that buildings never exceeded the height of the trees, he

asked why. He was told that buildings retain a human dimension. He thought this was an excellent idea.

The 150 hectares of land purchased by his father have since become a magnificent domain that has intentionally been left, as far as possible, in its wild state. For over forty years, the hotel has welcomed regular guests who have all fallen in love with the large rooms decorated with Moroccan, Indonesian, and Spanish objects, their magical view over the surrounding pine forest and the fabulous creek below. A fishing boat often comes here, microscopic amongst such a grandiose setting. In the kitchen, the young chef produces a new recipe every day, or nearly. Sabine has developed a biological crop project and prepares tea with herbs from the mountains. Tours and rambles are organized for guests to discover the island's superb flora and fauna. There are regular concerts in the

gardens. The atmosphere is warm and friendly. The madness of nights in Ibiza seems far away. Ten minutes from the hotel, the Sant Carles hippie market and its tents fragrant with incense, handmade articles and selection of embroidered tunics brings those flower power years alive again. Even nearer in the tiny village of San Gertrudis, you can experience again the Catalan atmosphere at the Costa bar with chorizo and Serrano ham served with a jar of sangria near the superbly illuminated church. Alvar dreams of executives working outdoors. He already has an idea. During the time the hotel was originally under construction, there was no road, no water, no electricity, and no telephone. The spirit of those intrepid dreamers who created Ibiza is still alive.

HOTEL HACIENDA - NA XAMENA
SAN MIGUEL, APARTADO 423
07080 IBIZA
SPAIN
RELAIS & CHÂTEAUX
TEL.: + 34 (971) 33 45 00
FAX: + 34 (971) 33 45 14
hotelhacienda@retemail.es
www.hotelhacienda-ibiza.com

53 rooms and 9 suites from $190 to $658.
El Sueño de Estrellas gastronomic restaurant,
Las Cascadas restaurant by the swimming pool,
Café de Paris bar, 3 swimming pools,
tennis court, fitness center, business center,
hairdressing salon, library…

How to get there
From Ibiza airport, follow the direction
of Ibiza-town for 4 km,
then the direction of Santa Eulalia -
San Juan. At San Miguel, take
the direction of San Miguel port,
and then that of the hotel,
located 2 km further on.

TAPROBANE
(SRI LANKA)

PAUL BOWLES

• TAPROBANE ISLAND •

View over former Ceylon, from the terrace of Taprobane Island.

"It was a whim but I fell in love with the island as soon as I set eyes on it", said the current owner, an Englishman who lives in Hong Kong. It is impossible to disagree with him. The picture is simply irresistible. It embodies in one place all the solitude, sunshine, fascination, mystery, and exube-rance so dreamt of by those in love with the islands. Therefore, in the same way as a thief reacts upon finally seeing that longed-for-jewel within his reach, you shiver with expectation as you near the place.

The island is a hundred meters away from the mainland, in Weligama Bay, to the southeast of Sri Lanka. At high tide, you may have to wade through the clear waters to reach it. Hence, the owner often recommends that his guests arrive wearing a swimming costume, carrying their clothes on their head. At low tide, however, you only need to take a short walk along the white beach. Once you have landed on the island, you will climb up a pretty white wooden staircase that soon disappears into the tropical greenery. Then follow a few stone stairs between the densely spaced trees. Just one more second and you have become part of the perfectly painted picture.

One house, the jungle, standing alone in the middle of the ocean. The beauty and absolute peace with nothing too pretentious or outrageous. The place is rented out, with its five bedrooms, refined objects, beautiful books, sculpted ceilings, delightfully shady verandah, divine swimming pool hewn out of the rock and its memories.

The solitary Paul Bowles, the cosmopolitan dandy, must have felt at home there, surrounded by characters who were nearly all like him, adventurers, tireless travelers, globetrotters who had made traveling their way of life. The writer spent the best part of his life in Morocco, but before that he lived in Paris, Mexico, the Algerian Sahara, Spain, Virginia and New York, where he was born. His incessant travels provide fuel for his stories and through his whole life he retained the nostalgia of long journeys, to the point that when someone asked him one day why he did not travel any more, he replied: "I don't travel any

Opposite and above: *Paul Bowles in 1969: work and play.*

more because there are no more boats". Long distance travel was a precious commodity to him. He brought back anecdotes from his trips and stories of people who could not be separated from the scenery surrounding them. One day, he discovered the island that he had always dreamt of: Taprobane. It belonged to the exiled French aristocrat, the Count of Mauny, who built a superb white colonial-style villa there in the Twenties. This took up a large part of the tiny piece of land at hand. The entrance is called The Hall of the Lotus because lotus flowers are depicted on the columns and on the ceiling. The bedrooms are spread around the hall, separated from it by curtains. A botanic garden surrounds the house. That is all there is of the island, minute and magnificent. From 1952 onwards, Paul Bowles divided his time between Taprobane and Tangier. "Sometimes", he said, "when I could not find a boat that stopped at Colombo, I had to go via Bombay. But that was quite fun in fact". He loved

Taprobane: all that Sri Lankan tradition.

the unexpected, those surprises that can turn a journey into a memory that belongs only to you. In Taprobane, he worked, wrote articles for magazines such as *Holiday*, had guests, the writer Arthur C. Clarke, author of *The Space Odyssey*, who settled in Sri Lanka also, or Peggy Guggenheim. She predicted he would not stay long, and that this adventure was beyond his means. Paul Bowles was plunged into a dream, in contrast to his wife Jane who was experiencing a nightmare. It was too hot. The wild nature distressed her. They only had an old oil lamp to light up the Hall of the Lotus. No point in even thinking about any sort of social life. She had absolutely nothing to do while Paul was shut up in a room working on his novel, *The Spider's House*. During a trip to Colombo, she sent a plaintive letter to her friend Tennessee Williams signed ironically "Spider Woman".

A month after her arrival on the island, she decided to leave. Paul Bowles stayed to finish his novel, and then started his crazy travels once again, Japan, Hong Kong, and Singapore. In 1956, he finally sold Taprobane. Peggy Guggenheim was right.

As you explore the house and its grounds, between the palm tree vegetation and frangipane trees, you will be unable to prevent yourself from thinking about the first people who discovered Sri Lanka, when it was still called Taprobane, and about all those who loved living there, who also settled themselves down on the terrace to look at the beach, the bay, and the garden. After all these years, the house has miraculously retained all of its charm, rare elegance, and extraordinariness. Only a few necessary improvements have been made, as well as the addition of a magnificent swimming pool. The current

owner, who is always ready for an adventure and is setting up his own elephant polo tournament, acquired the island by dint of patience. He had made an offer to buy it from the previous owner and was told that the place was not for sale. Some time later, the previous owner changed his mind and called him. It is difficult to remain insensitive to the perseverance required to acquire some possessions, or to the passion necessary to own some places. Taprobane is not an ordinary place. I asked the owner if he would sell it to me. He told me that the island was not for sale. A very good sign.

TAPROBANE ISLAND
C/o THE SUN HOUSE
23 UPPER DICKSON ROAD
GALLE
SRI LANKA
TEL.: + 94 (74) 380 275
FAX: + 94 (9) 22 624
taproban@sri.lanka.net
www.taprobaneisland.com

Rental of the island (5 rooms)
from $1,000 (during off-peak season)
to $2,000 (during peak season).
Library, swimming pool,
1 hectare of tropical forest, excursions…

How to get there
From the Colombo international airport,
travel to the south by car (allow 3 and a half
hours travel) to Weligama Bay. The island can
be reached from the coast quite simply
by putting your feet into the water,
or riding an elephant.

BAHAMAS
(ATLANTIC OCEAN)

"FOR YOUR EYES ONLY"

• PINK SANDS HOTEL RESORT •

The beaches of the Pink Sands Hotel Resort.

Jamaica, Cuba, the Greek Islands, Malta, Gibraltar, Sardinia, the Bahamas, Thailand… Where would James Bond be without these islands, without their golden coastlines fringed by swaying palm trees simply too good to be true, without these stunning sub-aquatic settings?

In *Thunderbird*, the Bahamas were already featured in prime position. Sean Connery met up again with Dominique, a charming creature portrayed by Claudine Auger. In *Never say Never* he had taken up service in the Bahamas and started out on the tracks of another fatally attractive beauty played by Kim Basinger. In *For Your Eyes Only* his partner was Greek, her name was Melina and the underwater scenes were shot in the superb depths of the great ocean.

Commissioned to trace the whereabouts of a British spy boat wreck, James Bond is also assigned to unmask the killers of a marine archaeologist. Carole Bouquet, as Melina, this archaeologist's daughter, was his accomplice during his adventure at Corfu, Cortina d'Ampezzo, the fantastic Météores monastery. Shooting started in September 1980 and precipitously dispatched 007 to 1001 different places. Of course he was assisted in this assignment by an unimaginable number of the most amazing gadgets of varying sorts and sizes, such as the yellow Deux Chevaux, which must have been quite a change for James and a far cry from his usual Aston

Martin; an astonishing two-seater mini-submarine called *Neptune*, especially made for the film by Peter Lamont, the Englishman who worked on numerous James Bond films before winning an Oscar for *The Titanic*. The famous marine photographer Al Giddings directed the underwater sequences. On board the *Neptune*, James and Melina set off to explore the wreck of the lost ship *St. George*. During the expedition, James was attacked by a giant diving machine, also built especially for the film, and found himself face to face with a shark that suddenly leapt out from the shipwreck. Al Giddings and his team, almost exclusively comprised of experts and professional deep-sea divers, fully portray the surrealist and frightening atmosphere. Peter Lamont did even better. He succeeded in convincing us of the existence of a Greek temple right

Line up of James Bond girls.

For your eyes only...

at the bottom of the ocean. In actual fact, everything was made in England and shipped out to the Bahamas. The actors were filmed on dry land, with powerful blowers to reproduce the effect of water in their hair, and fish tanks were shot in such a way as to give the impression of real sea. Amazingly astute inventions that made each and every James Bond film quite unique.

The Bahamas, near Jamaica, where Ian Fleming, the "author" of James, had his house, are in keeping with the Bond image with a chain of 700 islands and over 2000 smaller islands to the southeast of Florida, including Nassau, the most famous town. Lucayan Indians were the first inhabitants, well before Christopher Columbus discovered them. The pirate Black Beard made this port

Salon at the Pink Sands Hotel Resort.

his headquarters. Rum dealers during the American prohibition also did likewise. Tourists, for their part, discovered the Bahamas in the Thirties. Offshore from Nassau, the Nassau Scuba Center organizes deep sea diving to some of the locations visited by James Bond where remains of models used for some of the films can still be found, full of fish. Paradise Island, half an hour away from Nassau, is truly a location worthy of *Dr. No* with Versailles Gardens, an authentic French monastery from the 14th Century rebuilt stone by stone, and the famous Atlantis, an astonishing hotel cum theme park. There you can see the largest marine aquarium in the world, the reconstitution of a Mayan temple set in a tropical forest, and a giant transparent tunnel that crosses a shark infested lagoon! Nearby, in a much quieter setting, Harbor Island is a magnificent secluded location, just like those of which 007

was so fond, along with many other celebrities. The island is tiny, with narrow tree-lined roads, bordered by adorable pastel-colored houses bedecked with flowers and surrounded by white fences. All the charm of New England. Set in luxurious gardens, Pink Sands Hotel dominates the island's superb beach, a beach whose pink sands extend over 5 km and which is famous all over the world. The atmosphere is very relaxed here, elegant without any special effects. all the 25 cottages have a private patio and are scattered throughout a tropical garden with a view either overlooking the ocean or the luxuriant vegetation. The decoration combines Indian, Colonial, and Creole items. A swimming pool stretches out in the heart of the garden, with tennis courts and all the underwater activities you could possibly think of. Nothing is missing. Chris Blackwell acquired the hotel in 1992 and turned it

into an enchanting hideaway, which is continually extolled by glossy magazines, and where, for over forty years now, the most demanding clientele continue to be welcomed. In the local village, Dunmore Town, you can play dominos for hours on end. On Sundays, women dress up to go to church. At any time of day or night, men go out fishing in the sea and bring back conch, the Bahama Island shellfish that can be eaten either cooked in batter, in a soup, or in a salad. Hemingway, fond of these islands and of deep-sea fishing, once brought in a 223-kilo tuna. At the hotel, sitting in the Blue Bar by the beach, discriminating guests may take their time whilst smoking one of the magnificent cigars from the cellar, with a cocktail prepared with style by a barman whom James would most definitely have approved of.

PINK SANDS HOTEL RESORT
HARBOUR ISLAND
THE BAHAMAS
TEL.: + 242 333 2030
FAX: + 242 333 2060
pinksands@islandoutpost.com
www.islandoutpost.com/hotels/pinksands
/index.html

25 cottages
from $525 to $1,400 (during off-peak season),
and from $655 to $2,100 (during peak season).
Garden restaurant, Blue Bar,
swimming pool, 3 tennis courts, kayak,
diving, beauty center…

How to get there
From Nassau international airport,
take a domestic flight to North Eleuthera airport,
from where a cab will drive you to the hotel
in 20 minutes.

Opakaa Falls in Hawaii.

Jack London is quite incredible. At the age of twelve, he put his first boat on the water, a tiny little canoe, in San Francisco Bay. At fourteen he got a job with a fish preserving factory where he worked thirty-six hour shifts without a break, giving all his earnings to his mother, whilst dreaming of one thing only: to leave. To get away. As far as possible. He took the first opportunity to do just that, taking us with him on the most amazing journey that only he could have possibly imagined. Through the wildest scenery to offer us the most enchanting pages that travel writing has ever created. His preparation was not always ideal. Approximate information was no problem. It is this astounding freedom that is so fascinating.

His destiny led him one day to the islands. This took place during the legendary *The Cruise of the Snark*, a crazy scheme, as was often the case with him. Or rather, complete and utter madness, taking his wife Charmian and himself from Hawaii, to the Marquesas Islands, to Tahiti, to Fiji, to Australia. Inspiration came whilst chatting to a friend around their swimming pool at Glen Ellen. Why not have a fifty-eight-foot sailing ship built? Why not sail away for a trip around the world? A doddle for this former factory worker, docker, seal hunter, wanderer, rancher, and boxing journalist. Nothing frightened him, nothing stopped him. The success of *The Sea Wolf* partly financed the project, as well as numerous articles he produced at a frenetic rhythm throughout the cruise, sending them to magazines at each halt. At the end of April 1907, the couple left Oakland aboard the *Snark*. Professionals forecast a future lasting about ten minutes. They were not entirely wrong, but Jack London was obstinate and despite his far from perfect ship, it nevertheless held out for a year and a half. His wife Charmian recounted their adventures or rather, misadventures in a hilarious ship log, that inspired Jack London to write *The Cruise of the Snark*. As might be supposed, everything predicted did in fact take place. The ship did not hold water and broke down. Everyone on board was ill. The crew, who

HAWAII
(POLYNESIA)

JACK LONDON

• FOUR SEASONS RESORT HUALALAI •

Jack London on board the "Snark".

were ever changing, tore themselves away from the night-mare as soon as they reached the first stopover in Hawaii, where they arrived after twenty-seven days at sea, quite stunned at actually having reached terra firma. Their first sight of land was Oahu island, Honolulu and Waikiki Beach, as well as the volcanic slopes of Punch Bowl and Tantalus. Members of the Hawaiian Yacht Club came to meet them, but as the navigators had been at sea for nearly a month and the ship's roll had become an integral part of them, they were practically incapable of recovering their balance to walk to their hosts. Memories come tumbling out, amusing, moving and deliriously funny. Several pages recounted their first attempts at "surf riding" and Jack's rather promising débuts. Molokai island, Honolulu, the

Waikiki beach hotels, ukuleles, the ascent of the Haleakala volcano on Maui island, the speech Jack gave to the rich sugar cane growers about the revolution, one of his favorite subjects, and his idea of hiring a former jailbird as his new Captain. During the last two years of his life, Jack London spent most of his time there, using the islands' compelling beauty as a base for several short stories and novels.

Hawaii inspired him with more solemn tales, *The Lepers of Molokai* or *Island Stories,* that sought to break the postcard image, but *The Cruise of the Snark* remains a reference book, the story of an extraordinary expedition achieved by dint of enthusiasm and determination, but above all, an excellent guide of what not to do.

Of course things have changed, but Hawaii has retained

The Beach Tree Pool at the Four Seasons Resort Hualalai.

a certain charismatic craziness of its own and this is what makes it such an unusual place, famous the world over. Easy to imagine Harry Belafonte crooning *Matilda*. Bikini-clad girls on the Waikiki Beach. The Hawaiian shirt invented in the Twenties by a certain Ellery Chun. GIs sipping "Between the Sheets", and surfing and canoeing, the fascinating national water sports. The clichés are all there, remaining inexorably present. Nothing more impressive than surfers on the north coast of the Big Island, the surfers' Pantheon, trying to ride that perfect wave and disappearing into the jaws of breakers that can reach a height of over ten meters. Fantastic scenery abounds on Hawaii, the Big Island, and the largest of the eight islands that make up the Hawaiian archipelago. Volcanoes, lush forests, beaches and spectacular waterfalls, you will have to stray from the usual haunts to perceive

them, leaving behind Oahu, Honolulu and the beach in Waikiki that has now become full to bursting. The Big Island is home to the most active volcano in the world, a botanic park overrun with endemic animal and plant species, a fabulous coastal valley, Waipio Valley, a mixture of jungle, flowers and water-falls, and three main towns including Kona, where an impressive deep sea fishing competition is organized every year.

Near Kona, the incredible Four Seasons Resort Hualalai epitomizes everything that is so extraordinary about Hawaii. It is like a country all by itself: six swimming pools, an aquarium where you may swim with 3,500 tropical fish, four restaurants, a children's club, a famous golf course designed by Jack Nicklaus, a spa in the tropical gardens as a tribute to the cult of the body, so natural here. The walls are decorated with delightfully handcrafted pieces, canoe

paddles, necklaces of human hair and ivory. The bedrooms are evocative of Hollywood glamour. And behind the lobby, a cultural center offers countless activities to enable you to draw closer to Hawaiian traditions.

In 1778, the British explorer James Cook discovered these beautiful islands, already inhabited since 700 by the Polynesians who brought with them their culture and philosophy, which can be summed up today in the Spirit of Aloha, a welcoming and friendly manner of approaching life. One day in August 1971, it was the turn of spaceman James Irwin to discover these islands from a little higher up, aboard his space capsule Apollo 15 and he said: "After crossing the Pacific, we had permission to approach the moon. Then I looked out of the window and right down there, stretched out below, were the Hawaiian Islands, framed quite amazingly bang in the middle of my field of vision". Almost certainly magical.

FOUR SEASONS RESORT HUALALAI

100 KA`UPULEHU DRIVE,

KA`UPULEHU-KONA,

HAWAII 96740

USA

TEL.: + 1 (808) 325 8000

FAX: + 1 (808) 325 8200

www.fourseasons.com/hualalai/

243 bungalows (including 31 suites) from $675.
Pahv i'a restaurant, Beach Tree Bar & Grill,
5 swimming pools, spa, fitness center,
golf course and tennis court…

How to get there

From Kona international airport, take highway
n° 19 for 11 kilometers. Turn left at crossroads
and follow signposts.

BORA BORA
(FRENCH POLYNESIA)

"MUTINY ON THE BOUNTY"

• BORA BORA LAGOON RESORT •

The Bora Bora Lagoon Resort "farés"

Marlon Brando had always loved travel. He even considered globetrotting as "one of the main attractions of an
acting career" to the Rocky Mountains in Canada, Paris,
Rome, Monterey, Louisiana, Colorado, the Philippines,
Australia, and Tahiti, to go away, a change of scenery, see
something different. He even accepted roles because
he wanted to visit a particular place. During a trip to Bali,
he met a sailor who had decided to settle on the island.
"This man seemed to be living such a wonderful life"
he said, already fascinated.

In 1960, MGM offered him the part of Christian Fletcher
in a remake of *Mutiny on the Bounty*, in Tahiti. Ever since
his teens, when he had seen photos of the place in the
National Geographic magazine, he had always wanted to
go there. Above all, he remembered the incredibly serene
expression on people's faces. For some while now, he had
felt the need to find new meaning for his life. Tahiti came
along at the right time. "As soon as I saw Tahiti, reality
was greater than even my wildest dreams". He thought
the Polynesians were the happiest people in the world.
Shooting took place on a replica of the *Bounty*, anchored
just off the island. As soon as the film director yelled
"Cut!", the actor yanked off his uniform and jumped into
the water to swim with the Polynesian walk-on cast.
A movie like so many others, and yet another trip.
However, this time, a new life had begun for him during
the shooting of this motion picture.

One day a friend pointed out to him a piece of land on the
horizon. This was Tetiaroa. "It was not long before this
place had me under its spell, with a fascination that was
nearly mystical", he said. He learned that it belonged to
an elderly blind American lady, Mrs. Duran. He also
discovered that Somerset Maugham mentions it in one of
his books, that lepers once lived there and that it had been
the official residence of the Pomares, the Polynesian royal
family. Three deserters from the *Bounty* also landed there.
Very quickly caught, they received twenty-four to forty-
eight whiplashes and one month in irons for this
escapade. All this only increased his enthusiasm and
when someone suggested a meeting with Mrs. Duran, he
gladly accepted. Their encounter was a great success, and
he returned to visit the old lady several months later, this
time with an apple pie. Two or three years went by and
then one day, quite out of the blue, he received a letter
from Mrs. Duran telling him that she wanted to sell.

Lewis Milestone's mutineers.

Tarita Teriipaia, the Polynesian legend on screen.

Marlon Brando seized this chance. In 1966, he became the legal owner of Tetiaroa for ninety-nine years. "I promised her that I would not spoil the place and I have kept my word", he said. He built a little runway, houses for the Polynesians, a school and a tiny hotel "that never made any money". An air link was also set up between Papeete and the atoll but, as the actor remarked, "the most I can say is that there is no first class travel!" He later said that he owed his most wonderful memories to Tahiti,

and that he had come close to experiencing true peace and serenity there. "The world has lost any capacity to make people happy, too obsessed by modern comfort, by possessions. We have forgotten the simple pleasures of being alive". His life on Tetiaroa was as simple as could be. He read. He contemplated the scenery, the sky, and the stars. Above all, he had succeeded in disappearing.

The anonymity afforded by the islands is not an illusion. In 1790, the real mutineers who had returned to Tahiti

Preceding double pages: *Two Maori women portrayed in Gauguin's "primitive" works.*
Above: *The subdued natural interior of the Resort.*

after their rebellion took refuge on the island of Pitcairn. They were never found again. Far removed from all main routes, it is very easy to be forgotten.

Tahiti is one of those places that is far from everything, formed of legends, traditions that impregnate daily life, and those unchanging images, including the fabulous technicolor photography in the movie, "vahines" bedecked with flower necklaces that dazzled Christian Fletcher (Marlon Brando also married Tarita, his co-star in the movie), the famous Black Pearls, legendary dugout canoes or pirogues, farés on stilts like those in the Bora Bora Lagoon Resort, one of the splendid waterfront hotels on the Bora Bora lagoon. The modern response to the mutineers' dream. Typical farés with roofs covered in pandanus leaves and parquet floors in oiled yucca woods, aesthetic decoration, simply natural,

a mythical lagoon, with no neighbors on the horizon, an exquisite view of Mount Otemanu, the highest peak in Bora Bora, diving locations to take your breath away and all the magic of Orient Express legend in the heart of Polynesian enchantment.

Those who first went there, the Philippinos or Indonesians, who had undertaken that long and enduring journey that now takes just a few hours, were mesmerized. Tahiti and its islands also enchanted sailors, who found three things that they considered essential: "water, pigs and women". The island continues to bewitch and beguile. Because of the remoteness? The beauty? Yes, but also something else: The traditional hospitality and kindness so characteristic of the Polynesians' ever-present open friendliness and efforts to talk quite unaffectedly in the street, their courtesy and a sincere interest in others,

qualities rarely seen in cities and to which visitors are little accustomed. Yes, life on this side of the planet appears to advance quite independently from the rest of the world. On their dream motus, Polynesians live at their own rhythm, impervious to the obsessions of their congeners. During the shooting of *Mutiny on the Bounty*, a young girl in the movie wanted to go home to see her boyfriend. The producer reminded her of the contract that prevented her from going. The girl told him he could have her dog and two goats instead. He retorted that things did not work like that and that if she left, she would be arrested. She said, "Okay", and off she went. The script had to be reworked. Hollywood meant nothing to her.

PHOTOGRAPHIC CREDITS

BIBLIOGRAPHY*

Tu leur diras... [*You will tell them...*] by Maddly Bamy, Robert Laffont, Paris, 1999.

Songs my Mother Taught me by Marlon Brando and Robert Lindsey, Random House, New York, 1994.

My wiked wiked Ways by Errol Flynn, Buccaneer Books, New York, 1978.

The Cruise of the Snark by Jack London, The Macmillan and Company, New York, 1911.

Article on Henry Vere Stacpoole by Edward A. Malone of Missouri University.

Paul-Émile Victor ou l'Aventure intelligente [*Paul-Emile Victor or an intelligent adventure*]
by Marianne Monestier, Desclée de Brouwer, Paris, 1974.

Voyages d'artistes en Corse [*Artists and their Corsican travels*] by Jean-Marc Olivesi, La Marge, Ajaccio, 1993.

Mémoires du large [*Souvenirs of the deep*] by Éric Tabarly, published by de Fallois, Paris, 1997.

Five o'clock Angel: Letters by Tennessee Williams to Maria St Just by Tennessee Williams,
Penguin, New York, 1991.

*Non-exhaustive

ACKNOWLEDGMENTS

The author would like to thank Bertrand, her husband, who once again has proved a remarkable supporter and coach. She would also like to thank her publisher, Martine Assouline, and her team as wonderful as ever; Janie Samet, for her advice and her irreplaceable enthousiasm; her translator, Diana Stewart, as passionate as she is competent; Philippa and Eduardo Yrarrázaval for their precious memories of "La Bahia" and Philippa's inspired drawings; Alejandra di Andia and Joy, always there for me; Éric Laniesse, Manager of Actuel Voyages in Paris and his extraordinarily efficient team; Jean-Paul Gondonneau, Commercial Director of Turavion Tourismo, in Santiago, Chili ; Emmanuelle Friloux for her Polynesian assistance; Odile Lichon of Tahiti Tourisme; Barbara Bowers in Key West; Christelle Velut of OBT Com; Christine Causse of Ocean Futures Europe; Just Jaekin; Anez Taufik for her Bali assistance; Daniel Chun in Hawaii; Robin Rushnell at Martha's Vineyard. And of course, she would like to express all her gratitude to the island owners who welcomed her, to the hotel managers and press attachés who once again replied patiently to her innumerable telephone calls, e-mails, faxes, letters..., and to all her friends who gave her an idea, or two. Her thanks also to all those websites that provided her with information and her apologies to any authors and site managers that she may have omitted to mention.

The publisher wishes to thank AKG, Azienda Autonoma di Soggiorno e turismo delle Isole Eolie (Luciano Siracusa), Mrs. Belin-Capon, Collection Christophe L. (Serge Darmon), Corbis, Les Films du Losange, the Fondation Jacques Brel (France Brel and Bruno Tummers), the Fondation Monet (Mrs. Lindsey), Grégoire Gardette, Gla international, Keystone (Isabelle Sadys), Magnum (Marco Barbon), Martha's Vineyard Chamber of Commerce (Leigh Vayo), Photononstop (Patrice Huchet), RMN, Rue des Archives (Catherine Terk), Erik Staal, Armel Vialet, as well as Mrs. Yrarrázaval.

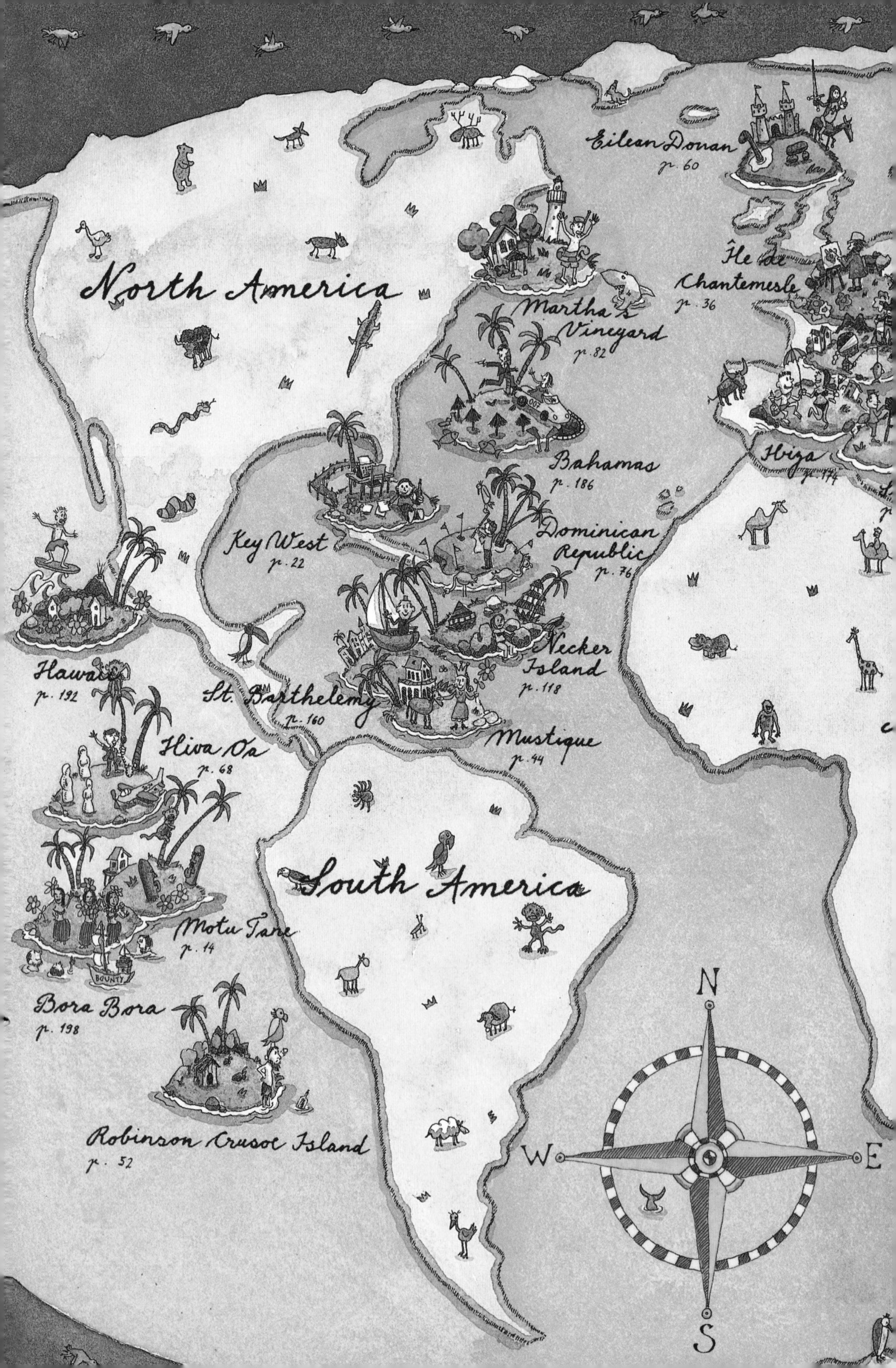
Eilean Donan
p. 60
Île de Chantemesle
p. 36
North America
Martha's Vineyard
p. 82
Ibiza
p. 174
Bahamas
p. 186
Key West
p. 22
Dominican Republic
p. 76
Necker Island
p. 118
Hawaii
p. 192
St. Barthelemy
p. 160
Mustique
p. 44
Hiva Oa
p. 68
South America
Motu Tane
p. 14
BOUNTY
Bora Bora
p. 198
N
W
E
S
Robinson Crusoe Island
p. 52